# Gardening
# Naturally

# Gardening Naturally

**Getting the Most from Your Organic Garden**

ANN REILLY

# MetroBooks

# MetroBooks

An Imprint of Friedman/Fairfax Publishers

© 1995, 1997 by Michael Friedman Publishing Group, Inc.

Library of Congress Cataloging-in-Publication Data

Reilly, Ann.

Gardening naturally : getting the most from your organic garden / Ann Reilly.

p.   cm.

Originally published : Demoines : Better Homes and Gardens, c 1993
Includes bibliographical references and index.
ISBN 1-56799-224-2  (hardcover)
1.  Organic gardening.   I.  Title.
[SB4353.5.R45   1997]
635'.0484--dc20                                    96-36401

Editor: Kelly Matthews
Art Director: Lynne Yeamans
Designer: Stephen Bitti
Photography Researcher: Daniella Jo Nilva

Color separations by Rainbow Graphic Arts Co., Ltd.
Printed in China by Leefung-Asco Printers Ltd.

10 9 8 7 6 5 4 3 2

For bulk purchases and special sales, please contact:
Friedman/Fairfax Publishers
Attention: Sales Department
15 West 26th Street
New York, NY 10010
212/685-6610 FAX 212/685-1307

Visit our website:
http://www.metrobooks.com

*To my mother and father, Rita and Rolf, who loved and nurtured me
the way a dedicated gardener loves and nurtures his plants.*

# ❧ CONTENTS ❧

INTRODUCTION     8

*Chapter One*
STARTING FROM THE GROUND UP: THE SOIL     14

*Chapter Two*
FERTILIZING YOUR GARDEN NATURALLY     32

*Chapter Three*
GROWING THE NATURAL GARDEN     50

*Chapter Four*
NATURAL INSECT AND DISEASE CONTROL     70

*Chapter Five*
THE NATURAL FLOWER GARDEN     98
    A DICTIONARY OF ANNUALS     116
    A DICTIONARY OF PERENNIALS AND BIENNIALS     126

*Chapter Six*
THE NATURAL VEGETABLE GARDEN     138
    A DICTIONARY OF VEGETABLES     148

*Chapter Seven*
THE NATURAL HERB GARDEN     160
    A DICTIONARY OF HERBS     170

SOURCES OF NATURAL GARDENING SUPPLIES     184

BIBLIOGRAPHY     185

HARDINESS ZONE MAP     186

INDEX     187

# INTRODUCTION

*A bountiful harvest travels from garden to table by balancing soil, fertility, pest control, and the crops themselves in a natural way.*

Rachel Carson's name might be best remembered for her 1962 book, *Silent Spring*. Taking a stand against pesticides and herbicides that were damaging the ecological balance of our earth, her position against the indiscriminate use of chemicals and the resulting pollution of the land and waters caused public outcry and increased awareness of the value of natural farming and gardening. In response to her warnings, DDT and a number of other toxic chemicals were eventually banned.

Although the overall use of insecticides has unfortunately increased since the publication of *Silent Spring*, a growing number of Americans has also realized the value of natural gardening, which permits no toxic chemicals to be applied to the soil or the plants.

Insecticides have been used by farmers and gardeners for many years. The oldest of these include pyrethrum and rotenone, which are plant-derived chemicals that do no harm to man and animals and are still in use today. Later, toxic chemicals based on mercury, arsenic, and nicotine were introduced, and during World War II, these were followed by DDT. New insecticides based on nerve gases and organic phosphates were introduced shortly thereafter.

Chlorinated hydrocarbons, which include the now-banned DDT and other close relatives, act on the central nervous system and can cause cell degeneration. Some of these chemicals are thought to be carcinogenic. Organic phosphates inhibit muscle and nerve response and were originally developed for use in chemical warfare. Some can be absorbed directly through the skin. It is no wonder that natural gardeners completely shun the use of these chemicals.

Toxic chemicals, however, have more deleterious effects. They can indiscriminately kill predatory insects, birds, fish, and other wildlife, upsetting the balance of

*The beauty of a mixed border will quickly convince you of what you can achieve with a natural garden.*

nature. This leaves harmful insects in an environment where they can thrive and multiply, because no natural checks and controls remain. In some cases, insects and diseases can also build immunity to chemicals, rendering them worthless.

Natural gardeners have become aware that with the selection of insect- and disease-resistant plants, proper soil preparation and maintenance, natural insect and disease control, and crop rotation, they can produce beautiful flowers and nutritious edible plants that are safe to eat but contain no harmful residual chemicals. These gardeners know they are not poisoning the air, the ground water, the soil, or themselves. They have also learned that naturally grown plants grow larger, stronger, and healthier, making them less attractive to attack by insects and diseases or at least better able to combat any attacks that might occur.

Gardeners who have been using chemical pesticides and fertilizers might wonder whether they can convert to a natural garden. Have I been using chemicals too long? Is it too late? The answer is a firm no!

However, don't expect to convert a chemical garden to a natural one overnight. It will take time, perhaps several years, to achieve the perfect balance, and disappointments may occur in the process. In the long run, better growing success will be achieved along with the certainty that the crops are healthier.

To correct soil laced with chemical residue, the only measure short of complete soil replacement is the application of activated charcoal at the rate of $3/4$ of a pound (340.1g) per 100 square feet (9 sq m) of soil. The charcoal will absorb and render harmless most of these residues. In addition, charcoal will improve drainage, and it contains minerals and other plant nutrients.

The next step in converting to a natural garden is soil improvement, which is outlined in chapter one. If the original planting is dense, it might be advisable to remove perennial plants from the ground, improve the soil, and then replant. As the soil is improved with amendments, fertilizer, and mulch, earthworms should start to thrive; if they are not present, they can be introduced. Introduction of beneficial insects, crop rotation, companion planting, and other good gardening practices that will help to achieve a totally natural garden are outlined in chapter four.

It is possible that until you have achieved a natural balance in the garden, you may have to resort to the use of chemical pesticides, but this should be done only as a last resort. When you have achieved your natural garden, you'll discover that chemicals are unnecessary.

This book outlines principles of natural gardening that can be applied to the growing of any type of plant. The main focus, however, is on the growing of annual and perennial flowers, vegetables, and herbs, plants that are primarily grown from seed and that die completely or to the ground in autumn after the first frost (these are sometimes called herbaceous plants). An in-depth discussion of trees, shrubs, or bulbs is not included, although the basic principles of soil preparation, fertilizing, and garden care can be applied to these types of plants.

Whatever plants you are growing, you will be pleasantly surprised with the results achieved with natural gardening. If it sounds hard to believe, try it yourself. Once you have, you'll never want to abandon the principles of natural gardening and will quickly become a natural gardening proponent, expounding its benefits to all your gardening friends.

# Chapter One

# Starting from the Ground Up: The Soil

© Anita Sabarese

*You'll never underestimate the value of natural fertilizer once you compare a fertilized lettuce plant (ABOVE LEFT) with an unfertilized one (ABOVE RIGHT).*

Although flowers, vegetables, and herbs will grow in any reasonably good soil, they will thrive so much better in an improved, organic soil that it is worth making the effort to fine-tune it. If you need proof, try growing identical plants side by side in unimproved and improved soil. You'll be so amazed at the more vigorous plant growth, health, flowering, fruiting, and resistance to insects, diseases, and drought that occur in the improved soil that you'll never question the value of a highly organic soil again.

The best growing medium for plants is soil that is fertile, moisture-retentive, and rich in organic matter. Soil like this almost never occurs by itself; most often it is the product of careful tending over the years.

However, no amount of fertilizing, watering, pampering, or attention paid to plant selection will grow a beautiful and productive garden unless you start properly from the ground up—with a good soil.

To create the best possible conditions for plants, you'll almost always have to adjust your soil. To do this, you'll need a basic understanding of soil and its properties and how they are related to growth.

## ■ SOIL TEXTURE AND SOIL STRUCTURE

Soil is composed of mineral particles of sand, silt, and clay, which exist in varying proportions depending on the type of soil in your garden. Sand particles are largest (0.2 to 0.05mm), clay particles are smallest (0.002mm or less), and silt falls in between (0.05 to 0.002mm). The size of the soil particles determines what is known as soil texture; the arrangement of the particles is referred to as soil structure. Almost no soil is composed entirely of particles of one size; most are a mixture of these particles plus organic matter, air, and water.

Plants growing in sand must be watered and fed frequently, because soil that is too sandy dries out quickly and cannot retain fertilizer. Fertilizer leaches, or washes, through it rapidly and thus needs frequent replenishing. On the positive side, the coarse texture and loose structure of sand provides the aeration needed for good root growth, and its fast-draining qualities help keep it relatively free of soilborne diseases.

*A healthy vegetable garden (LEFT) starts from the ground up in an organic soil that is fertile and moisture-retentive.*

*Loam (RIGHT, TOP), the solid portion of ideal soil, is a combination of sand (CENTER), clay (BOTTOM), and silt.*

© Derek Fell

17

*A rich soil, ready for planting, crumbles easily in your hand.*

*© Lynn Karlin*

### ■ SOIL AMENDMENTS

Since good loam rarely occurs naturally, and since its organic content will probably be less than ideal, your soil will most likely need improvement with one or more soil amendments. Soil amendments are not the same thing as fertilizers. Fertilizers supply nutrients, and amendments improve the soil's structure, drainage, aeration, and nutrient and water retention. However, many soil amendments also supply nutrients and neutralize acidity or alkalinity, and some organic fertilizers, such as cottonseed meal and sewage sludge, have soil-amendment value.

### ■ ORGANIC SOIL AMENDMENTS

Organic matter in the form of decomposed animal or plant material—often called humus—is the most valuable and versatile amendment you can apply to your soil. Added to clay soil, it makes the soil coarser and thus more airy and fast-draining. Added to sandy soil, it helps retain moisture and nutrients. In any type of soil, organic soil amendments give the soil a more loamlike texture and proper balance of solid matter, moisture, and air.

Heavier clay soil holds water and nutrients well, but usually has poor drainage because the tiny air spaces between its small particles do not allow water to pass through easily. Because of clay's fine texture and dense structure, aeration is also poor.

Silt, ranking between sand and clay in particle size, has both the good drainage of sand and the nutrient-holding capacity of clay. Silty soil is also extremely friable, or easy to work. It is an excellent soil for growing plants, but rarely occurs naturally; it is usually mixed with sand and clay.

The solid mineral portion of the most ideal soil, which is known as loam, is a mixture of 30 to 50 percent sand, 30 to 40 percent silt, and 8 to 28 percent clay, in proportions that equal 100 percent. Like silt, loam drains well yet retains enough water to promote growth. It has good aeration, allowing roots to absorb oxygen and giving them room to grow, and it has excellent nutrient-retaining properties. Loose and friable, good loam is composed of 50 percent solids (mineral particles plus organic matter), 25 percent air, and 25 percent water.

In addition to improving soil structure, organic matter helps supply the soil with nutrients by promoting the growth of microorganisms that convert soil nitrogen into a form roots can absorb. These same organisms aid in eliminating or controlling harmful, soilborne disease organisms. Some organic soil amendments can also supply nutrients—although usually at a level so low that additional fertilizer is needed (see chapter two). Organic matter also provides food for earthworms, which assist in aeration. Many forms of organic matter are acidic in nature and help to lower soil pH (its level of acidity or alkalinity) as well;

*Compost, one of the best natural soil conditioners, can be prepared in a bin,* *which, as shown below, can do double duty as the base for a cold frame.*

© Derek Fell

others are alkaline and raise soil pH. In hot and dry climates, generous amounts of organic soil amendments are a must to retain soil moisture and protect plants from damage from heat.

There are many sources of organic soil amendments for the garden. Among the most popular are sphagnum peat moss, leaf mold (shredded and composted leaves), shredded or ground bark, dehydrated manures, wood ashes, and compost. Some are sold at garden centers, others are available in agricultural areas, and compost can be made inexpensively in a backyard compost pile. Refer to the following chart of organic soil amendments, which outlines the basic similarities and differences. Your choice should be guided by this, as well as by local availability and cost. Please note that the three sets of figures used in the chart for each fertilizer value refer to the percentage (by weight) of nitrogen, phosphorus, and potassium, respectively. The next chapter fully explains these three elements and the role they play in gardening.

# 🌿 *Organic Soil Amendments* 🌿

■ **COMPOST**
**Moisture retention:** Good
**Nutrient retention:** Excellent
**Fertilizer value:** 1.5 to 3.5–0.5 to 1–1 to 2
**pH:** Usually acidic
**Comments:** Easy to make at home

■ **COW MANURE**
**Moisture retention:** Good
**Nutrient retention:** Good
**Fertilizer value:** 0.50–0.30–0.50
**pH:** Usually alkaline
**Comments:** Best used dried

■ **LEAF MOLD**
**Moisture retention:** Excellent
**Nutrient retention:** Excellent
**Fertilizer value:** 0.8–0.35–0.15
**pH:** Slightly acidic
**Comments:** Oak leaves are best; chop before use

■ **HORSE MANURE**
**Moisture retention:** Good
**Nutrient retention:** Good
**Fertilizer value:** 0.7–0.3–0.6
**pH:** Usually alkaline
**Comments:** Best used dried

■ **SPHAGNUM PEAT MOSS**
**Water retention:** Excellent
**Nutrient retention:** Excellent
**Fertilizer value:** 1.5 to 3–0.25 to 0.5–0.5 to 1
**pH:** Acidic
**Comments:** Moisten before incorporating into soil

■ **STEER MANURE**
**Water retention:** Good
**Nutrient retention:** Good
**Fertilizer value:** 0.25–0.15–0.25
**pH:** Usually alkaline
**Comments:** Contains weed seeds and salt

■ **TREE BARK**
**Water retention:** Good
**Nutrient retention:** Good
**Fertilizer value:** 4–2–4
**pH:** Slightly acidic
**Comments:** Use only shredded or ground bark for
soil amending

■ **WOOD ASHES**
**Water retention:** Good
**Nutrient retention:** Good
**Fertilizer value:** 0–1.5 to 3–5 to 7
**pH:** Highly alkaline
**Comments:** Use only in sandy soils

Plants side-dressed with compost (ABOVE) receive nutrients as well as protection from temperature extremes, splashing water, and weeds.

Irises (LEFT) thrive with a top dressing of leaf mold, which contributes large amounts of organic matter to improve the structure of all types of soil.

## How to Make Your Own Compost

Compost is decayed organic material used to condition the soil; it is one of the best soil amendments and one of the least expensive. In addition, it is an excellent way to recycle kitchen and garden waste.

Compost is created when organic waste materials properly decompose. The decomposition is aided by bacterial microorganisms that get their energy by digesting dead and decaying organic material and cause the organic matter to become finely decomposed. These same microorganisms, when later incorporated into the garden soil, can reduce or stop the action of harmful soil-disease organisms.

These microorganisms need a blend of protein (for nitrogen) and carbohydrates to perform their task. High-protein waste includes kitchen scraps, grass clippings, and coffee grounds. High-carbohydrate wastes are dry autumn leaves, straw, and sawdust. Both types of materials are necessary for a successful, quick-acting compost pile. Manures can also be added to the compost pile.

To make a compost pile, select an out-of-the-way place (for appearance's sake). The pile can be made in a mound, a pit, or a variety of enclosures such as garbage cans, wooden boxes, or open bins. The size of the compost pile is limited only by the space available, the amount of material you have to place in it, the amount of organic matter you need for the garden, and the time you have to devote to it. The minimum size for a compost pile should be 3 feet (0.9m) wide by 3 feet (0.9m) deep by 4 feet (1.2m) high. If

© Charles Mann

© Liz Ball/Photo/Nats

space is not a problem, it can be larger, but if it is any wider or deeper than 5 feet (1.5m) or taller than 6 feet (1.8m), it will probably be difficult to turn the compost inside. If compost is made in a container, be sure there are holes in it for drainage and aeration.

Some composting structures use double or triple bins to hold compost in varying stages of decomposition. Since compost is best when made in a batch instead of by continually adding new material to a working pile, these double or triple bins come in very handy.

The rate of decomposition will be increased if the items placed in the compost pile are ground or chopped up first.

The easiest way to start a compost pile is to alternate a layer of protein source with a layer of carbohydrate source. As the material decays, it becomes hot; when the temperature at the center of the pile reaches 140° to 150°F (60° to 66°C) (check the temperature with a meat thermometer), the pile should be turned. If the pile is decomposing properly, this should be done every three to five days. Four to six turnings are usually needed to complete the cycle. If the pile does not get hot enough, it will need nitrogen from a protein source or from a nitrogen fertilizer. Manure, a

*Compost (TOP LEFT) can be made in an open pile or in any type of structure ranging from a fancy bin to a simple enclosure of chicken wire. A soil thermometer (BOTTOM LEFT) can be used to gauge when to turn a compost pile.*

good source of nitrogen, can also be added to the compost pile.

Organic compost activators are available at garden centers and through mail-order sources. Although there should be enough bacteria present to activate a compost pile, these products are an insurance policy. Follow label directions regarding application.

When turning a pile, place the material that was in the center of the pile on the outside, and move the material that was on the outside to the center. This assures uniform decomposition. Turning the pile also aerates it, as oxygen is needed by the microorganisms to complete their task. Water is needed too, but too much water is detrimental as the microorganisms can't survive if they're too wet. Water only when the pile is dry. If the pile starts to develop an unpleasant odor, it is too wet; lessen the amount of water applied and cover the pile with plastic or a tarp if it is rainy.

When the compost is ready, it will be dark and crumbly, its components will not be recognizable, it will have cooled down, and it will have shrunk to about half its original size.

Organic matter decomposes best in a neutral pH, so add limestone, ground oyster shells, egg shells, or wood ashes to neutralize the acidic qualities of organic wastes.

The heat of a compost pile usually destroys disease organisms, insects, and weed seeds, but it is best not to add any material that is infected, infested, or has weed seeds present.

## ■ GREEN MANURE

Green manure is a term applied to certain cover crops that are grown in the garden during the off-season and then plowed or turned into the soil while they are still green. This is an excellent way for natural gardeners to improve poor and compacted soil, although it may take several years for maximum improvement to be achieved. Green manure adds organic matter and nutrients to the soil and may also loosen the soil, depending on the crop. If space permits, half of the garden can be planted with green manure for an entire year to improve the soil even more.

There are basically two types of cover crops used for green manure. The legumes, especially peas, beans, clover, alfalfa, and vetch, fix nitrogen in the soil, increasing its nutrient content for later crops as well as adding organic matter to the soil. If you choose legumes, be sure to inoculate the seeds with nitrogen-fixing bacteria at planting time. This bacteria is available where seeds are sold, and some legume seeds are sold already inoculated.

The other type, crops like wheat and rye, have extensive root systems and are excellent for loosening the soil and improving its structure. They also add organic matter to the soil when plowed or turned under. Like wheat and rye, clover is a good choice for its soil-loosening properties.

Either type of cover crop, or both, can be planted. Planting should take place in autumn, about two months before the first frost, with turning under done the following spring, before planting.

## ■ SHEET COMPOSTING

Sheet composting is similar to green manuring, the difference being that with sheet composting, the plants are grown in a different part of the garden. They are then laid on top of the soil to be improved and either covered with a layer of soil 1 to 2 inches (2.5 to 5cm) thick, or plowed or turned into the soil. Between growing seasons, the plant material decomposes.

## ■ EARTHWORMS

The presence of earthworms is the sign of a loose, rich, fertile soil. Natural gardeners encourage earthworms for their beneficial contributions to the growing

*After your peas are har-*
*vested and shelled, turn the*
*plants into the soil; being*

*legumes, peas also increase*
*the soil's nitrogen content*
*while they are growing.*

scheme. As they move about, they loosen and condition the soil. Their droppings have fertilizer value as
well. If your garden does not have earthworms, you can
buy them at some garden centers or through the mail.
If they do not survive, it means that your soil needs
further improvement.

## ■ INORGANIC SOIL AMENDMENTS

There are times when the use of a natural but inorganic
soil amendment is called for. The most common of
these are gypsum, coarse builder's sand, perlite, and
vermiculite. Gypsum, or calcium sulfate, is an inorganic
compound that is often used to improve the structure
of heavy clay soil that does not drain well. It binds the
small clay particles together into larger clusters that
allow air and water to penetrate the soil more
effectively. Gypsum is also effective in treating the
alkaline soils of arid areas. In addition to improving the
soil structure, it forces toxic sodium in these soils to
leach out. Since gypsum is a neutral salt, however, it
will not change the soil's level of acidity or alkalinity,
and you must therefore add other amendments if soil
pH needs adjusting.

Gypsum is usually sold in fifty-pound (22.6kg)
bags at garden supply stores, in either granular or
powdered form. Use 10 to 20 pounds (4.5 to 9kg) per
100 square feet (9 sq m) of garden space, spreading it
over the soil each spring and watering it in.

Coarse builder's sand, perlite, and vermiculite,
like gypsum, are mixed with the soil when it is being
improved for planting. Unlike gypsum, which reacts
chemically with the soil, their action is purely physical.
The best material to use will depend upon the type of
soil you have; check with the horticulture department
of your area's cooperative extension office or your local

garden center or garden club to find the best solution
for your area. Any of these amendments may be mixed
into the soil until they reach a maximum volume of 20
percent of the final solid soil component.

Builder's sand is useful for coarsening fine clay soil
to improve its drainage and aeration. It is available in
bags or in bulk from building supply stores or from
outlets that sell concrete and cement. Be sure to use
only coarse sand; fine beach sand will not improve
drainage and will actually do more harm than good
because of its small particle size. When mixed with clay,
fine sand will turn the soil into cement. The addition of
sand will not affect the pH of the soil.

Perlite and vermiculite are often added to soils to
improve their structure without changing their pH;
each is available in bags at garden supply stores. The
one you choose will depend on the type of soil you
have in your garden. Perlite, a grayish-white granular
material, is mined from volcanic lava flows and is heat-
processed. Its lightweight, porous texture improves the
drainage of heavy clay soils. However, it has no
nutrient value.

Vermiculite, on the other hand, contains some
magnesium and potassium and is an excellent retainer
of other nutrients as well. This granular material is
mined and then subjected to high heat, which makes
it porous and capable of holding very large quantities
of water and dissolved nutrients. It is therefore not
recommended for heavy clay soils—which already
retain water and nutrients effectively—but it will
improve the performance of sandy soil.

Never think that inorganic soil amendments are to
be used as a substitute for organic soil amendments.
They do, however, have some desirable characteristics
when used in conjunction with organic materials.

## ■ SOIL TESTING

Since there is no way to be sure what kind of soil you have by looking at it, it's a good idea to have your soil tested every year or two. This can be done by a private soil-testing laboratory (check the yellow pages or advertisements in gardening magazines) or with soil test kits available at garden centers or supply stores. The kits tend to be less accurate than testing done by laboratories. Most cooperative extension offices also offer testing by university laboratories.

Soil test kits usually measure pH only and thus may not reveal any other, potentially serious defects in your soil. The tests done by laboratories are more complete, indicating not only pH, but also the soil texture, the amount of organic matter, the major and minor nutrients present, and the level of plant toxins present, and will often include the corrective measures you need to take.

The symptoms of excessively high or low pH are very similar: yellowing leaves, lack of proper growth and flowering, and in severe cases, the death of the plant. The only certain way to distinguish too-high from too-low pH is to test the soil. Nutrient deficiencies also have visible characteristics, but these are often similar, and soil testing is the only way to determine these also.

## ■ PH

A soil's acidity or alkalinity—measured by its pH level—is a characteristic that is independent of soil texture and structure but is just as essential to good plant growth.

The pH of soil is expressed on a scale of 0 to 14, with lower numbers indicating acid soil and higher numbers indicating alkaline (basic) soil. A pH of 7.0 is neutral. Soil pH varies from region to region, depending on local soil chemistry, water table levels, and rainfall. In general, areas with high rainfall have acid soils in the 4.5 to 7.0 range, and arid regions have alkaline soils with a pH of 7.0 to 8.0.

In a soil that is too acidic or too alkaline, plant nutrients become insoluble and cannot be absorbed by the plants' roots. At the same time, toxic elements are more soluble and can potentially kill the plants or severely damage their roots. Moreover, beneficial soil bacteria will not grow in either highly acidic or highly alkaline soil.

Most annuals, perennials, vegetables, and herbs grow best at a pH of 6.0 to 6.5. In this slightly acidic range, most of the nutrients that plants need are readily available. Those annuals and herbs that tolerate neutral to slightly alkaline soils include dusty miller, geranium, vinca, pinks, and thyme. Many vegetables will also tolerate a slightly alkaline soil.

## ■ RAISING THE PH OF ACID SOIL

If a soil test indicates that the pH of your soil is too low, you can raise it by adding limestone (calcium carbonate). Ground dolomitic limestone, calcium magnesium carbonate, is the best to use because it also contains magnesium, an element essential for plant growth. If this is not available, use ground agricultural lime (calcium oxide), but stay away from hydrated lime (calcium hydroxide), which can burn plant roots. Apply limestone to the surface of the soil, mix it with the top few inches of soil, and saturate the area with water. Soil pH should be corrected prior to planting, and treatments will need to be repeated every few years, when testing shows it is required.

To raise the pH from 4.5 to 6.5, apply limestone at the rate of 10 pounds (4.5 kg) per 100 square feet (9 sq

© Anita Sabarese

*Dusty miller prefers a neutral soil (pH 7.0); adjust the pH as necessary with limestone, ground oyster shells, wood ashes, or sulfur.*

© Anita Sabarese

*Geraniums prefer a slightly acidic soil with a pH of 6.0 to 7.0*

m). If the pH is 5.0, use 7 pounds (3.2kg) of limestone per 100 square feet (9 sq m). If the original soil has a pH of 5.5, 5 pounds (2.2kg) of limestone will be needed to raise the pH to 6.5. To raise the pH from 6.0 to 6.5, use 3½ pounds (1.6kg) of limestone per 100 square feet (9 sq m). These rates apply to sandy soils. Use an additional 20 percent for clay soils and an additional 10 percent for silt or loam soils, since the particles in these soils are finer and there are more of them. However, you should apply no more than 5 pounds (2.2kg) per 100 square feet (9 sq m) at one time. If more is needed,

wait a month before reapplying. Be prudent when applying limestone; using too much can render trace elements insoluble and thus unavailable to plants.

Ground oyster shells can also be used to raise pH. They, like limestone, contain calcium carbonate, but because they have a coarser consistency, they are also useful in loosening the soil. Wood ashes will also raise soil pH, and these contain beneficial amounts of phosphorus and potassium as well. Be careful when using wood ashes, however, because overuse can cause burning.

*A large bed is prepared by tilling in a cover crop of rye.*

© Lynn Karlin

## ■ LOWERING THE pH OF ALKALINE SOIL

If your soil is too alkaline, you can lower its pH by adding agricultural sulfur. It is sold in powder form in bags, boxes, or cans at garden or agricultural supply stores. To apply, spread it over the soil, dig it into the top several inches, and then water.

To reduce the alkalinity of a sandy soil from 8.0 to 6.5, use 2.5 pounds (1.1kg) of sulfur per 100 square feet (9 sq m). Apply 1.5 pounds (0.7kg) per 100 square feet (9 sq m) to reduce alkalinity from 7.5 to 6.5 and ²/₃ pound (0.3kg) to reduce it from 7.0 to 6.5. For silt or loam soils, double the rate; triple it for clay soils.

Use a maximum of 2 pounds (0.9kg) of agricultural sulfur per 100 square feet (9 sq m) per application. If a second or third application is needed, wait a month between applications.

Most humus and many fertilizers have a slight acidifying effect on soil, so if your soil is neutral or slightly alkaline, its pH may not need any further adjustments after amendments have been added. After applying one or more of these amendments, recheck your soil's pH to determine whether the acidifying effect has been sufficient. If it has not, add sulfur as necessary. It is wise to avoid alkaline organic soil amendments if the soil has a high pH to begin with.

Soil that is extremely alkaline is often difficult to correct. The best way to grow plants under these conditions is in raised beds or in containers.

## ■ IMPROVING YOUR SOIL

Once both a physical inspection and a soil test have been completed and you are aware of the deficiencies of your soil, the next task is to begin improving it. First you should decide whether to improve an entire planting bed

or just the soil in individual planting holes. Preparing an entire bed may be more work, but in poor soil, it is almost a necessity. It's also a necessity if you're starting plants outdoors from seeds and more practical if you're planting annual flowers, vegetables, or herbs. If you don't prepare the entire bed, you'll have roots that are trapped in pockets of ideal soil and surrounded by poor soil, which will eventually retard or damage their growth. If the soil in your garden is relatively good, however, you can usually get away with improving only

the soil in the individual planting holes, especially if you are planning to add perennials to an existing bed or border.

Whether you are improving a large bed or just the soil in individual holes, the procedure is the same. First, dig out the soil in the area to be planted to a depth of 8 to 12 inches (20 to 30cm). If you're adding trees or shrubs to your garden, prepare the soil to a depth of 16 to 24 inches (40 to 60cm). Use a hoe to break up clods of earth. Add to this 25 percent by volume of such

organic matter as sphagnum peat moss, leaf mold, dried manures, or compost. If you are preparing an entire bed, spread the organic matter over the area and work it in well to its dug-out depth. If you are digging individual holes, remove the soil from the hole and mix the organic matter with it. After combining the soil and the organic matter, the final mixture will have a larger volume than it did previously; raising the level of the bed in this way is actually beneficial to the plants because it improves drainage.

When incorporating organic matter, add a source of phosphorus such as bone meal or rock phosphate at the rate of 3 to 4 pounds (1.35 to 1.8kg) per 100 square feet (9 sq m). Phosphorus, which is essential for good root growth, moves very slowly through the soil. If it is applied to the top of the soil, it may take several years to filter down to the root level where it is needed. The best way to get it there is to put it there to begin with.

Adjust the pH if necessary at this time. If there are any rocks, stones, root fragments, or other pieces of debris in the soil, remove them. Combine the soil, organic material, phosphorus source, other fertilizers, and any pH-adjusting materials, and mix them well; in larger areas, a Rototiller will be helpful in breaking up large clods of soil and mixing in the soil-improving ingredients. If you are preparing a large bed, rake the soil level before planting.

It's best, although not always practical, to improve the soil one to six months before planting, because this allows the soil to mellow and settle, allows the pH to become properly adjusted, and lessens the chance that fresh organic matter or fertilizers will burn the roots of new plants. If the soil is improved in advance, add pH-adjusting materials one month before adding fertilizers.

Soil should never be improved unless it is in workable condition; that is, fairly dry and friable. Working with soil that is too wet will ruin its structure by binding its particles together, and these will be difficult or impossible to break apart in the future. To test the workability of your soil, pick up a handful and squeeze it into a ball. If the soil sticks together, it is too wet. Wait several days and try again. Soil is ready to be worked when it crumbles in your hand when you squeeze it. If the soil is so dry that it is fine and dusty, water it well first and then retest it before working it.

## ■ DRAINAGE AND AERATION

Good soil drainage is essential for almost all plants. If drainage is too slow, water will replace air in the soil, taking the place of oxygen that is vital for root growth and leaving roots no room to develop. Ideally, the space between soil particles should be half water and half air. When sufficient air is present in the soil, it is said to have proper aeration.

To test your drainage, dig a hole about a foot (30cm) deep and a foot (30cm) wide. Fill it to the top with water, and keep track of how long it takes for the water to drain. If the hole empties in an hour or less, your drainage is fine. But if water remains longer, you'll need to take steps to improve the drainage. In many cases, simply mixing organic matter, gypsum, or one of the other soil amendments into the soil will be sufficient to correct a drainage problem. After working this material into the soil, repeat the test. If your soil fails again, you'll need to take more serious steps.

One solution is to add several inches of coarse gravel below the bottom of the prepared soil. Alternatively, you can dig a large trench beneath the planting bed and install drainage pipes or tile at the bottom of the trench. The gravel, pipe, or tile should be slightly pitched to take the water to a lower spot where it can drain off or into a sump, sewer, or dry well.

Another attractive solution to poor drainage is to build a raised bed. Using redwood, cedar, pressure-treated pine, railroad ties, landscape timbers, brick, or stone, construct a planting bed about 12 to 24 inches (30 to 60cm) above ground level. Add an improved soil or purchase a high-quality topsoil or soil-less mix (the latter is usually a mixture of peat moss and perlite or peat moss and vermiculite and can include sand and compost), and work it in with the soil below grade to a

© Derek Fell

depth of 18 to 24 inches (45 to 60cm), adding other amendments as necessary to achieve proper organic content, soil structure, and pH.

There are other advantages to raised beds. You won't have to bend over as far to weed or perform other gardening chores, and in spring, the beds will warm up faster than the surrounding soil, causing growth to begin earlier. Raised beds are also an excellent way to deal with extremely acid or alkaline soil.

## ■ DEALING WITH PROBLEM SOILS

Certain types of soil plague gardeners with chronic problems. An excess of salts in the soil in such arid areas as the southwest United States can stunt growth, burn foliage, or kill plants. Its presence can be detected by white deposits of salt visible on the surface of the soil.

The solution is the addition of gypsum to the soil coupled with deep, slow watering, which will flush the salt out of the root zone.

Another problem can be hard pan, which is an impervious layer of soil at or near the soil surface. Roots, nutrients, and water cannot penetrate it. Sometimes power equipment can break it up, but the best solution is the incorporation of generous amounts of organic matter into the soil.

Soil improvement is not something that can be done overnight. In fact, it is unlikely that it can be successfully completed in a year. You will need to be patient. In approximately four to five years, you will undoubtedly be proud of the soil that you and Mother Nature have created and pleased with the performance of the plants growing in it.

*Chapter Two*

# FERTILIZING YOUR GARDEN NATURALLY

© Lynn Karlin

*A combination flower and vegetable garden brings out the best of both when plants receive the proper nutrients.*

All plants need food in order to survive, grow, bloom, and fruit successfully. Although some nutrients are available naturally in the soil and air, supplemental fertilizing is essential if you want your plants to perform their best. The fertilizer you apply must not only be of the right formulation for your plants but must also be applied in the right amounts at the right times. In this chapter, you'll learn about the nutritional components of fertilizers, the value of natural fertilizers, how and when to apply fertilizers (instructions for incorporating fertilizer into the soil before planting are given in the previous chapter), and how to recognize nutrient deficiencies.

## ■ FERTILIZER BASICS

Fertilizers contain three elements that are basic for plant growth: nitrogen, phosphorus, and potassium (abbreviated N, P, and K, respectively). Nitrogen stimulates early spring growth and promotes deep green color and root, stem, and leaf growth. Phosphorus is necessary for a plant to produce sugar during photosynthesis, and it encourages root growth and flower and fruit production. It also strengthens stems, helps in resistance to pests and diseases, and increases the rate of vegetable crop maturity. Potassium helps regulate the plant's metabolism and contributes to early growth, stem strength, hardiness, vigor, good flower color, and disease resistance. It is essential for the proper development of root crops. A fertilizer containing all three of these elements is said to be a complete fertilizer.

All fertilizer formulations are expressed by a series of three numbers. The first is the percentage (by weight) of nitrogen; the second the percentage of phosphorus; and the third is the percentage of potassium. For example, 5–10–5 is 5 percent nitrogen, 10 percent phosphorus,

© Charles Mann

© Lynn Karlin

and 5 percent potassium. A fertilizer whose formulation is 0–3–2 has no nitrogen but contains 3 percent phosphorus and 2 percent potassium.

Flowers, herbs, and vegetables grow best when the fertilizer used has nitrogen, phosphorus, and potassium in a ratio of approximately 1:2:1, 1:2:2, or 2:3:1. The relatively lower proportion of nitrogen keeps the plants from producing lush foliage at the expense of flowers, fruits, and vegetables. Typical formulations of complete fertilizers are 5–10–5, 5–10–10, and 8–12–4. Those fertilizers used for lawns (10–6–4 is a common formulation) have a relatively higher proportion of nitrogen to promote leaf-blade growth and should not be used on flowers, herbs, or vegetables.

You often hear fertilizers referred to as "organic" or "inorganic." Organic fertilizers contain carbon and may be either natural or man-made. Natural organic fertilizers, such as bone meal, cottonseed meal, and fish emulsion, are minimally processed animal or vegetable by-products. Other organic fertilizers, such as urea, IBDU (isobutylidene diurea), and sulfur-coated urea, are manufactured from organic materials by synthetic methods. Natural gardeners should shy away from these because they are often harmful to the soil. Rock powders, although not organic, are a product of nature and are as essential to the natural gardener as truly organic materials. Natural fertilizers of all types take the form of particles, granules, powders, or liquids.

*Naturally grown and fertilized vegetables (LEFT) will complement any meal.*

*This wheelbarrow full of natural fertilizers (RIGHT) is a must for a successful vegetable garden.*

© Derek Fell

Inorganic, or chemical, fertilizers are man-made products containing no organic elements. They are manufactured from mineral salts, typically potassium nitrate, ammonium nitrate, ammonium phosphate, ammonium sulfate, calcium nitrate, potassium chloride, and potassium sulfate. These fertilizers are solids in their pure form but are often sold in solution.

Although both natural and chemical fertilizers supply plants with the same nutrients, and even though chemical fertilizers usually have a higher nutrient content, there are good reasons why natural gardeners will use only natural or organic fertilizers. Chemical fertilizers are highly water soluble and release nutrients to the plant quickly, but they leach through the soil rapidly and must be applied more often than natural fertilizers. A good deal of their nutrients are wasted in this leaching. Because they are very concentrated, they may burn plants if not used properly. Also, their component salts can accumulate in the soil over time, causing damage to the soil, to the plants that grow in it, and possibly to the groundwater. Chemical fertilizers have no soil-amending properties and can also increase a plant's susceptibility to disease.

It is true that natural organic fertilizers are bulky and that many do not contain as high a concentration of nutrients as inorganic or man-made organic fertilizers. Because they are natural, the exact proportions and amounts of nutrients may vary from batch to batch. Most do not have the right proportions of nutrients on their own, but they can easily be combined or supplemented with other fertilizers. The primary advantages of organic fertilizers are that they are slower to leach from the soil, they improve soil structure, they encourage the buildup of beneficial soil organisms, and they leave no residue of harmful chemical salts. A few

organic fertilizers, including seaweed and fish meal or emulsion, are rich in trace elements (see the section of trace elements that appears later in this chapter); seaweed also produces or stimulates plant growth hormones and increases plants' ability to withstand light frosts. Dried banana peels, which are very high in potassium, have become popular lately as a natural fertilizer.

## ■ CHOOSING A NATURAL FERTILIZER

Garden centers and other suppliers of fertilizers often sell ready-to-use complete natural or organic fertilizers. If you can't purchase these or if you don't wish to use prepackaged complete fertilizers, you can feed your plants a variety of natural fertilizers that will supply all the essential nutrients.

Because the components of natural fertilizers often vary, it is impossible to predict the exact proportion of nutrients that will be present in a given batch. However, the following analysis of common natural fertilizers shows the percentages of nitrogen, phosphorus, and potassium that are typical of each. Among those in the following list, the ones most commonly sold are blood,

© Lynn Karlin

bone, cottonseed, and fish meals, fish emulsion, and sewage sludge. Chicken manure is sometimes sold; if you live near a farm, you can collect it yourself. You can make arrangements with your local lumberyard to haul away their sawdust. Processed seaweed is becoming more available all the time. You'll probably have to eat your own bananas to get the peels, but the potassium in them is good for you too. Wood ashes, which are also discussed in chapter one under soil amendments, are a good source of phosphorus and potassium, and if you have a fireplace (or a neighbor with one), you will have a vast supply of them.

You will note that some fertilizers are slow to react, others release their nutrients at a medium rate, while still others are fast-acting. Fast-acting fertilizers are good when you want to see rapid results, but they are not a

*The seaweed mulch on these pepper plants provides nutrients (especially potassium), encourages benefi-cial soil bacteria, increases yields, and builds insect and disease resistance.*

permanent cure. They leach from the soil quickly and need replenishing often. Because of this factor, however, they are good for container plants, which need to be watered frequently and therefore lose much of the fertilizer applied to them. Fertilizers with a slow to medium rate of action are the best for long-term results.

Also note the pH of the various natural fertilizers, and take this into consideration when choosing one. It would not be wise to use wood ashes on an alkaline soil, since wood ashes are highly alkaline and would compound the soil pH problem. On acid soils, however, they are an excellent choice. Likewise, a fertilizer that is acidic would be the best choice for alkaline soils. When acidic fertilizers are used on acidic soils, some other material that is alkaline in nature (limestone, crushed oyster shells) must be added to adjust the pH to its proper level.

All else being equal, a fertilizer that has soil-amendment properties will be more beneficial over the long run than one that does not. However, the use of high-phosphorus fertilizers, such as bone meal and rock phosphate, is still essential, even though they have no direct soil-amending value. These fertilizers are best used at or before planting time to get phosphorus into the root zone. When choosing between rock phosphate and bone meal, be aware that bone meal decomposes much more slowly than rock phosphate.

Phosphate fertilizers such as rock phosphate work much better in a highly organic soil because the micro-organisms present in the soil utilize the phosphorus for a while and then release it for use by the plants. This process does not happen as quickly in a soil with low organic content, which means it takes longer for the plants to utilize the phosphorus in the fertilizer. Natural gardeners avoid the use of superphosphate, which is rock phosphate that has been treated with sulfuric acid, because it contains harmful salts and causes an imbalance in the soil microorganism population.

Remember that most natural fertilizers are slower to act than inorganic ones, so do not expect overnight results. Natural fertilizers rely on microorganisms to break them down into forms that plant roots can absorb, and this takes time. However, after several years of soil amending and natural fertilizing, your soil will be so good that you may need less fertilizer each year, and your larger, healthier plants and vegetables will be something you can boast about. Also, you'll be proud that your gardening efforts did nothing to spoil the balance of Mother Nature.

## Manure Tea

A valuable liquid fertilizer can be made by extracting the nutritional components from manure into water, and using the solution to water and fertilize plants. Using anything from a 5-gallon (19l) pail to a 50-gallon (190l) drum, soak a bag of cheesecloth containing horse or cow manure in water for 24 hours. The resulting solution will be dark brown or black. Dilute it further with water until it is the color of weak tea. After watering your plants, pour the solution onto the ground around them for quick fertilizing results. Use a proportion of approximately one part manure to three parts water. The residual manure can be incorporated into the soil or mixed into the compost pile.

# Natural Fertilizers

■ **BANANA PEELS**

**Fertilizer value:** 0–2.5 to 3–42 to 50

**Rate of action:** Medium to fast

**pH:** Alkaline

**Soil-amendment value:** High in beneficial bacteria

**Comments:** Dry before use

■ **BLOOD MEAL**

**Fertilizer value:** 12 to 15–0 to 1.5–0 to 1

**Rate of action:** Medium to fast

**pH:** Slightly acidic

**Soil-amendment value:** None

**Comments:** Also often used to deter animals from the garden

■ **BONE MEAL**

**Fertilizer value:** 0 to 6–12 to 27–0 (raw)
0 to 4–12 to 34–0 (steamed)

**Rate of action:** Slow (raw)
Slow to medium (steamed)

**pH:** Alkaline

**Soil-amendment value:** None

**Comments:** Steamed bone meal is less likely to burn than raw bone meal

■ **CHICKEN MANURE**

**Fertilizer value:** 6–4–3 (15 percent moisture)

3–2.5–1.5 (30 percent moisture)
1.5–1–0.5 (75 percent moisture)

**Rate of action:** Medium to fast

**pH:** Usually alkaline

**Soil-amendment value:** Retains moisture in sandy soil

**Comments:** Use carefully to avoid burning

■ **COFFEE GROUNDS**

**Fertilizer value:** 2.0–0.4–0.7

**Rate of action:** Medium

**pH:** Acidic

**Soil-amendment value:** Aids water retention in sandy soils

**Comments:** Easily accessible at no cost

■ **COTTONSEED MEAL**

**Fertilizer value:** 6 to 7–2.5–1.5 to 1.7

**Rate of action:** Slow to medium

**pH:** Acidic

**Soil-amendment value:** Good moisture retention

**Comments:** Avoid using on seedlings to avoid burn

■ **FISH EMULSION**

**Fertilizer value:** 5–1 to 2–1 to 2

**Rate of action:** Fast

**pH:** Acidic

*Wood ashes.*

**Soil-amendment value:** None

**Comments:** Needs frequent reapplication

### ■ FISH MEAL
**Fertilizer value:** 8 to 10–4–0

**Rate of action:** Slow

**pH:** Acidic

**Soil-amendment value:** None

**Comments:** Especially useful on root vegetables

### ■ ROCK PHOSPHATE
**Fertilizer value:** 0–20 to 32–0

**Rate of action:** Slow

**pH:** Alkaline

**Soil-amendment value:** None

**Comments:** Excellent for use at planting time to get phosphorus into the root zone; contains many trace elements

### ■ SAWDUST
**Fertilizer value:** 4–2–4

**Rate of action:** Very slow

**pH:** Acidic

**Soil-amendment value:** Loosens heavy clay soil

**Comments:** Needs to be used with a high-nitrogen fertilizer mixed into it; also used for mulch (see page 63)

### ■ SEAWEED
**Fertilizer value:** 1.7 to 3–0.8 to 1–5

**Rate of action:** Fast

**pH:** Acidic

**Soil-amendment value:** Encourages beneficial soil bacteria

**Comments:** Good for root crops; may increase insect and disease resistance

### ■ SEWAGE SLUDGE
**Fertilizer value:** 2 to 6–1.5 to 7–0.8 to 1

**Rate of action:** Slow

**pH:** Acidic

**Soil-amendment value:** Loosens heavy clay soil; good moisture and nutrient retention in sandy soil

**Comments:** Avoid use on food crops

### ■ WOOD ASHES
**Fertilizer value:** 0–1.5 to 3–5 to 7

**Rate of action:** Fast

**pH:** Very alkaline

**Soil-amendment value:** Good water retention in sandy soils

**Comments:** Do not use around young seedlings

*To avoid foliage burn, do
not spray liquid fertilizers
on foliage if temperatures
will exceed 90°F (32°C).*

Keep in mind that natural soil amendments have some fertilizer value (see chapter one for an outline of these and their relative nutrient value.)

Because the nutrients in many natural fertilizers do not occur in ideal proportions—indeed, some nutrients may be absent altogether—it is often useful to combine two or more of these fertilizers to achieve the right balance for the garden. For example, a combination of four parts (by weight) blood meal, four parts bone meal, and one part banana peels would give sufficient amounts of all three nutrients in an 8–12–6 ratio. Four parts coffee grounds, one part

bone meal, and one part wood ashes mixed together will result in a formulation which has a 12–24–10 ratio. All it takes is simple arithmetic—adding together their nutrient values—to figure out how much of each component you need.

## ■ HOW AND WHEN TO FERTILIZE

Proper timing is essential when applying fertilizer, because nutrients must be present in the soil when the plants need it most. This critical time is when plants are at their most active stage of growth and flowering. If fertilizer is applied too early, it may be partially leached from the soil before the plants need it. Applied too late, it may not be available on time.

The timing of fertilizer application will vary with the climate, but with perennial flowers, vegetables, and herbs it starts with the first signs of growth in late winter or early spring and lasts until cool autumn weather slows growth. With annual flowers, vegetables, and herbs, this critical time covers the entire growing, flowering, and fruiting period.

Fertilizer must also be applied in the proper amount, which depends on the type and size of the plants, the length of the growing season, possible competition from other plants, and the soil. Larger plants generally need more fertilizer than smaller ones, and those with a long growing season, such as potatoes, would likewise need more fertilizer than those that grow quickly, such as radishes. A yearly soil test would let you know for sure the nutrient content of your soil and what fertilizing recommendations are best for your garden.

If the soil pH needs to be adjusted, it should be done about a month before fertilizing to create the optimum pH for most plants, which is 6.0 to 6.5. Once the proper pH has been reached, nutrients are more

readily available for root absorption. This will also make your fertilizer go further. (For information on adjusting pH, see chapter one.)

Most natural fertilizers are dry fertilizers, although there are some natural organic liquid fertilizers, such as fish emulsion. Concentrated seaweed extracts are also sold in liquid form. These liquids are further diluted and poured or sprayed onto the soil around the plants and can also be sprayed on the foliage if the temperature does not exceed 90°F (32°C) (or foliage burn will occur). Because of their water solubility, they are faster-acting than dry fertilizers. But because they are fast-acting and because fertilizers leach quickly from containers, liquid fertilizers are best for container-grown plants.

Liquid fertilizers must be applied often if they are used on garden plants—as frequently as once every two weeks—since they release nutrients and leach from the soil quickly. They are therefore not as convenient to use in the garden as dry fertilizers and are usually used only as a supplement.

Mixing many gallons of liquid fertilizer for a large garden can be a time-consuming and backbreaking job. An easy alternative is to make a concentrated solution of fertilizer and use a device called a proportioner (or siphon) to siphon out the fertilizer with the water from a garden hose at the proper dilution. The proportioner attaches to the end of the hose and siphons small amounts of concentrated fertilizer from a bucket to mix with outgoing water. Proportioners are sold at garden centers and come with full instructions. You can also purchase special sprayers that fit on the end of a garden hose and dilute concentrated fertilizer solutions as the product is applied. These work in the same way as proportioners.

*Beds should be prepared with fertilizer either before or at planting time.*

To keep from burning the roots, always apply any type of fertilizer to moist soil, spreading it over the entire area under which roots are growing. Generally, this is the soil under the spread of the plant. Be careful not to spill dry fertilizer on the leaves or stems because it will burn them; if you do so accidentally, wash it off. Work the fertilizer lightly into the top of the soil with a trowel or a hand-held cultivator and water again.

When applying slow- to medium-acting fertilizers during the growing season, it is best to move any mulch aside, lightly scratch the fertilizer into the ground with a hand-held cultivator, and move the mulch back. Unless the fertilizer is in contact with the soil, it will not work properly.

Perennial flowers, vegetables, and herbs should be fertilized in early spring when signs of growth appear. Annual flower, vegetable, and herb beds should have fertilizer incorporated either before or at planting time. Whether or not a plant needs additional fertilizer during the growing season depends upon what type of plant it is. If beds were properly prepared before planting, additional fertilizing may not be necessary unless you notice that growth and flowering are poor or that the foliage appears to be nutrient deficient. If you harvest an early crop of vegetables, you should add more fertilizer before planting a late crop in the same place. In chapters five, six, and seven, which discuss flowers, vegetables, and herbs, it is noted what plants need additional fertilizing after early spring feeding or bed preparation.

Many experts now recommend dormant feeding for perennials and woody plants, which is the application of fertilizer during the late autumn or winter when the plant tops are not growing. Since roots continue to grow in autumn and winter as long as the soil temperature stays above 40°F (4°C) and start to grow in spring

Courtesy Sporty's Tool Shop Catalog

phosphorus, and 0.1 to 0.4 pounds (.05 to .18kg) of potassium, unless a soil test has shown that you have a deficiency of one of the essential elements, in which case more should be applied.

Since fertilizers leach more rapidly from sandy soils than they do from other types of soil, they may need to receive fertilizers more often. If you see signs of reduced growth or nutrient deficiency, either correct the soil with more natural soil amendments or shorten the interval between fertilizer applications by about one-third. When plants are grown close together, they may need about 20 percent more fertilizer if they show signs of reduced growth.

It is important not to use a complete fertilizer on perennials or woody plants later than two months before the first autumn frost; using it any later will encourage new growth on the plants that will not have time to "harden off" or adapt to the cold weather before winter chill can damage it. However, a fertilizer that contains little or no nitrogen but has phosphorus and/or potassium (such as bone meal, rock phosphate, or dried banana peels) can be applied in early autumn. Phosphorus and potassium will help the plants adapt to cold weather, lessening dieback and other injuries that can occur during winter. Phosphorus and potassium fertilizers can also be worked into beds that will be planted in the spring to give them time to decompose and be more available for uptake by the roots.

If foliage turns crisp and brown, it is a sign that you may have overfertilized, although this is very unlikely with natural fertilizers. Water the plants heavily to leach excess fertilizer out of the ground, and adjust future feedings to keep the problem from recurring. You can do this by trial and error or, better yet, by having your soil tested.

before top growth appears, fertilizer supplied during the dormant period will already be in the soil for the roots to absorb when they can use it. If perennial and woody plants are dormant-fed in autumn or winter, an early spring application of fertilizer is not needed. In warm areas, where plants grow all year, dormant feeding will not be needed unless the plants are artificially forced into dormancy.

If you have purchased a complete fertilizer, always follow the direction on the label regarding the amount of fertilizer to apply, since this will vary with the formulation. It takes only half as much 10–10–10 fertilizer as 5–10–5 fertilizer to provide plants with the same amount of nitrogen and potassium. (The increased amount of phosphorus will do the plants no harm since phosphorus moves so slowly through the soil.) If you have made your own fertilizer out of separate natural components, apply it so that each 100 square feet (9 sq m) of growing area receives approximately 0.2 pounds (.09kg) of nitrogen, 0.3 to 0.4 pounds (.14 to .18kg) of

*Soil test kits (LEFT) are available at garden centers and supply stores.*

*Chlorosis (BELOW) is an iron deficiency in plants that results in yellowed leaves or leaves that will stay green only along the veins and can be permanently corrected only by changing the pH of the soil.*

## ■ TRACE ELEMENTS

In addition to nitrogen, phosphorus, and potassium, plants require small quantities of ten other elements, called trace elements, for proper growth. These elements are boron, calcium, chlorine, copper, iron, magnesium, manganese, molybdenum, sulfur, and zinc. Most already exist in sufficient amounts in the soil, water, or air, but a few—namely calcium, magnesium, sulfur, and iron— may need to be supplemented occasionally because they are lacking in most environments. Sometimes they are present in fertilizer formulations; check the label to be sure. Otherwise, you will have to use an alternative source. Deficiencies of the others are possible but rare; the chart on page 49 outlines deficiency symptoms, but only a soil test can confirm these for sure.

Plants use calcium for root growth, the production of strong stems, and the building of proteins. Common sources are regular or dolomitic limestone, gypsum (also a source of sulfur), crushed oyster shells, or crushed eggshells. Limestone, gypsum, and crushed oyster shells can be purchased at garden centers, and egg shells can be collected from your own kitchen or a neighbor's. Limestone, gypsum, and crushed oyster shells are used as soil amendments as well; limestone raises the pH of the soil, and gypsum is neutral to acidifying in highly organic soils. Crushed oyster shells raise soil pH as well as loosen compacted soil.

In addition to containing calcium, dolomitic limestone also contains magnesium, the basic element in chlorophyll that enables plants to utilize other nutrients, especially nitrogen, phosphorus, and sulfur. Magnesium is essential for leaf and protein production.

Sulfur promotes root and top growth, helps maintain a dark green color, and is also used to acidify the soil. It is present in gypsum, and powdered agricultural

sulfur can be purchased at garden or agricultural supply stores. It is wise to check the soil pH after pure sulfur is added to the soil to make sure that it hasn't lowered the soil pH too much.

Iron is needed for plants to produce chlorophyll and carbohydrates; if it is lacking (or in alkaline soil, present but unavailable), leaves will turn completely yellow or will stay green only along the veins. This is called chlorosis. In highly organic soils, the microorganisms present help to dissolve soil iron and make it available to the plants. A solution of chelated iron, a powder or liquid sold at garden centers, can also be sprayed onto plants if chlorosis occurs. Since iron in alkaline soils is chemically unavailable to plant roots,

also check the pH of the soil and correct it if necessary. Applying chelated iron to alkaline soil is only first aid; adjust the pH to permanently correct the deficiency.

In addition to the special supplements already mentioned, many general-purpose fertilizers also supply trace elements. If present, these elements will be listed on the label and will probably be sufficient to cure all but extreme deficiencies. It is also possible to buy mixtures containing some or all of the ten trace elements. Garden centers and agricultural supply stores are sources of these. Follow the label for application rates and frequency of application.

## ■ DIAGNOSING NUTRIENT DEFICIENCIES

If your plants are not growing as well as you think they should be, the cause may be a nutrient deficiency. The following table lists common symptoms of the lack of major and minor nutrients; minor nutrients are rarely lacking in a soil with proper organic content as long as the pH is in the correct range. The best way to confirm a suspected deficiency is with a complete soil analysis, available through your area's cooperative extension office or a private soil-testing laboratory. If the report indicates no problems with the soil, but the plants are still growing poorly, the next step is to determine whether you have an environmental problem, an insect problem, or a disease problem. (See chapter three for an outline of plants' growing needs. Chapter four contains a complete discussion of insects and diseases.)

A perfectly structured, highly organic soil amended with natural fertilizers is the best support you can give your plants to achieve strong growth, bountiful flower and fruit production, and the ability to ward off the effects of insects, diseases, and drought.

*This tomato plant displays signs of nutrient deficiency —poor growth and yellowing of leaves.*

# Symptoms of Nutrient Deficiencies

■ **NITROGEN**: Yellowing of older lower leaves, followed by browning and dying; slow or stunted plant growth.

■ **PHOSPHORUS**: Stunted plant growth; dull foliage with reddened undersides; purplish leaves and stems; small or few flowers or fruits.

■ **POTASSIUM**: Leaves turn yellow at the tips and between veins; leaves curl under; dry, black, or brown dead spots develop in yellow areas; lower leaves become dry; fruit is misshapen or yields are low.

■ **CALCIUM**: Terminal buds die; young leaves have a light green edge; older leaves become dull, may curl at the margins, and the leaf margins turn brown; stems weaken; blossom end rot develops on tomatoes.

■ **MAGNESIUM**: Yellowing between veins of older lower leaves, starting at the leaf tips and proceeding toward the middle, followed by browning and dying; leaves are thick and brittle; plants are stunted and produce little new growth.

■ **SULFUR**: Yellowing of older leaves without browning and dying; stems are slender and brittle.

■ **BORON**: Young leaves are light green on the bottom edge of the leaf; leaves are thick and roll up at the edges; flowers wither or terminal buds die back.

■ **CHLORINE**: Rarely if ever deficient, and its deficiency symptoms are not understood by soil and plant scientists.

■ **COPPER**: Young leaves wilt and turn yellow; stem tips are weak.

■ **IRON**: Young leaves are yellow except for main veins; then entire leaves yellow but do not turn brown. Symptoms start at top of plant.

■ **MANGANESE**: Lighter green areas develop between veins in young leaves; brown, dry, dead areas develop on leaves; plant growth becomes stunted.

■ **MOLYBDENUM**: Similar to nitrogen deficiency (see above); leaves also tend to be narrow and elongated; plant growth is stunted.

■ **ZINC**: Older leaves turn yellow in an irregular pattern, then turn bronze and eventually die; flower buds do not form.

# Chapter Three

# GROWING THE NATURAL GARDEN

© Stephen Bilti

*Baskets for collecting flowers, vegetables, and herbs are an asset to the "tool" collection.*

Achieving a beautiful and productive garden is not difficult. The previous two chapters have already explained how to prepare, enrich, and fertilize the soil. Add to that the proper guidelines for selecting the right plants to meet the climate and other environmental conditions, deciding whether to start with seeds or actual plants, planting, watering, mulching, weeding, providing winter protection if necessary, and manicuring the garden, and you will be able to create a natural garden that you will be proud of. No doubt your friends and neighbors will be impressed; and when they ask you how you did it, you'll be doubly proud to say that it is completely naturally grown. Don't forget the next chapter on controlling pests and diseases to round out your knowledge of growing a successful natural garden.

## ■ THE TOOLSHED

Whether you are a seasoned natural gardener or just a beginner, you will need certain basic tools for your gardening tasks. When you shop for tools, choose the best that you can afford. They will work better and last longer. Make sure to clean, sharpen, and oil them after use to prevent rust and to keep them in tip-top shape.

The basic toolshed for growing flowers, vegetables, and herbs should contain the following equipment.

■ **Asparagus knife**—for harvesting asparagus and for removing deep-rooted weeds.

■ **Grass shears**—to trim the lawn around beds, borders, the sidewalk, and fences.

■ **Hedge clippers**—to trim hedges and soft-stemmed plants. There are both manual and electric types available.

■ **Hoe**—for weeding.

■ **Pruning shears**—to cut woody stems and remove faded flowers.

■ **Rakes**—one with rigid tines to level beds and borders before planting; another with flexible tines to rake leaves.

■ **Shovel**—for planting and moving soil, mulch, fertilizers, and so on.

■ **Spade**—for digging, mixing soil, and working in soil amendments and fertilizer.

■ **Spading fork**—for digging perennials and other large plants; for breaking up clumps of soil.

■ **Sprayer**—to apply pesticides and fungicides.

■ **Spreader**—to distribute dry fertilizers.

■ **String trimmer**—power trimmer to replace grass shears.

■ **Trowel**—for planting or digging small plants.

## ■ SELECTING THE RIGHT PLANT FOR THE RIGHT PLACE

Before starting any garden, you'll need to make the basic decision of what plants you'd like to nurture in it. Part of that decision depends, of course, on the type of flowers you're partial to or which vegetables and herbs

*The ultimate tool shed—
well equipped, clean, and
organized.*

*The flavor of brussels sprouts improves with frost —they can be harvested after the first snowfall.*

© Lynn Karlin

you'll want to use in the kitchen. But the decision goes much further than that. If the plants you select aren't compatible with your climate, all the pampering in the world won't make them grow properly, if they even grow at all.

The chapters on flowers, vegetables, and herbs specifically outline the various environmental requirements for different plants. Study these before you order seed packets or buy plants. If your climate is hot, melons would be a better choice than brussels sprouts, and sunflowers better than calendula. Likewise, cool climates will foster the growth of pansies and radishes, but not necessarily portulaca or okra.

Pay attention to light requirements. Some plants like full sun, while others grow best in partial or full shade. Water, too, is essential. If your climate is dry and

you don't have sufficient water to irrigate the garden, choose a plant that likes dry soil and/or tolerates drought. Where rainfall is high, select plants that like moist conditions.

## ■ GROWING PLANTS FROM SEEDS

Many gardeners buy annual flowers, vegetables, and herbs as bedding plants in the spring because they lack the time and/or the space to grow their own plants from seeds. Many others, however, enjoy starting seeds indoors in the winter and early spring. It's economical, enjoyable, and sometimes the only way to grow the specific varieties you want for your garden. Although many seeds can be sown directly into the garden, others require direct sowing, so starting these seeds indoors gives your garden a head start and ensures earlier blooming and fruit production.

The first thing you will need to grow seeds indoors is a container. You can purchase flats made from compressed peat moss or plastic or make your own containers from milk cartons, aluminum baking pans, or frozen-food dishes. A container can be any size but should be 2½ to 3 inches (6.25 to 7.5cm) deep to allow for proper root development.

The two basic requirements for containers are that they be absolutely clean and have drainage holes in the bottom. If you are reusing a container, wash it well with soap and water, and rinse it with a 10 percent solution of household bleach in water. Never reuse a container made of compressed peat moss for sowing seeds, because you will not be able to ensure its cleanliness and it could introduce disease organisms.

Large seeds and seeds that are difficult to transplant should be sown into individual containers made of plastic or compressed peat moss. The roots will be

*A greenhouse in spring
(BELOW) is bursting with
plants waiting to be moved
to their new garden home.*

disturbed very little during transplanting, especially when containers of compressed peat moss are used, because the entire container can be planted. The most common plants that require this special handling are anise, beefsteak tomatoes, borage, California poppy, caraway, chervil, coriander, corn, creeping zinnia, cucumber, dill, fennel, flax, lavatera, love-in-a-mist, lupine, melon, morning glory, nasturtium, parsley, phlox (annual), and poppy.

Sowing seeds is one aspect of gardening where an organic medium is essential. Sowing medium can be purchased, or you can make it yourself. You can use sphagnum peat moss by itself or a mix of half sphagnum peat moss and half perlite or vermiculite. Compost or leaf mold can be screened until it is fine in texture and then be used as well. Never use soil from the garden for sowing seeds indoors because it will not drain well, it has poor aeration, and it may also carry insects, diseases, and weed seeds.

Most seeds of annual flowers and herbs are started indoors six to eight weeks before the outdoor planting date, while most vegetables need five to seven weeks. The exceptions to this are noted in the specific chapters on flowers, vegetables, and herbs. Perennials vary in the time it takes for them to be ready for transplanting from seed, as explained in the chapter on flowers.

To sow seeds, place premoistened sowing medium into a container to within $1/4$ inch (0.6cm) of the top. To prevent a disease known as damping off, which causes the seedlings to suddenly topple over and die, use only clean containers and organic sowing media that has not been used before. Sphagnum peat moss is excellent because it has an acidic pH that inhibits the growth of the damping-off fungus. To further reduce the chance of this disease, do not overcrowd or overwater seedlings.

You can plant several types of seeds in the same flat, but they should all have the same light requirements and take approximately the same time to germinate.

It will be easier to handle seedlings if seeds are sown in rows, but this will be difficult for small seeds, which can be scattered over the surface of the medium. Except for those seeds that require light to germinate (these are specified in the list on page 58) and fine seeds, cover the seeds with enough moistened medium so that they are completely covered. Seeds that require light to germinate and fine seeds should not be covered, but rather should be pressed into the medium with your hand or with a fine spray of water.

Be sure to use a sowing medium to completely cover those seeds that require darkness to germinate (these are listed on page 58), unless they are fine seeds. Since fine seeds should not be covered with medium, place the container in a black plastic bag, cover it with a box top, or do something creative to block all light until germination occurs.

*Seedlings grown in individual pots are easier to transplant into the gar-* *den because their roots are less disturbed during the process.*

Some seeds, because they have a hard seed coat, require that they be soaked in warm water for 24 hours before sowing or that the seed coat be filed or nicked with the edge of small scissors or shears (if the seed is large enough to handle). Some annuals and many perennials require a cold treatment (stratification) before sowing to simulate winter and break the dormancy of the seed (see the listing on page 59 of the seeds that require special attention). To do this, place the seeds in moist sphagnum peat moss in the refrigerator or freezer for at least six weeks or sow the seeds outdoors in autumn for spring germination.

Most seeds can be stored from year to year, provided they are kept cool and dry. A few exceptions to this, which are seeds that are not long-lived and should therefore not be stored, are angelica, delphinium, geranium (perennial), gerbera, kochia, and salvia (annual).

After the seeds are sown, place the entire container into a clear plastic bag (except, of course, those seeds that need darkness to germinate). Position the covered container in good light but not full sun, and give it bottom heat to increase germination. Bottom heat can be achieved with either purchased heating cables or by placing the container in a warm spot, such as the top of the refrigerator.

There are a few seeds that require cool temperatures to germinate, and these should not be subjected to bottom heat. These can be germinated in a cool room or greenhouse or outdoors in early spring (see the list of these on page 59).

Until the seeds germinate, they should need no care. If excessive moisture accumulates on the inside of the bag, open it and let the medium dry out slightly. After the seeds have germinated, remove the plastic bag and place the container in full sun or under fluorescent lights that are turned on for 12 to 16 hours a day. Once the seedlings have developed two sets of true leaves (the first growth you'll observe is not true leaves but leaflike structures called cotyledons, which are used for food storage), they should be thinned out or transplanted into individual containers containing soil-less medium so their roots have enough room to grow.

During the growing period, keep the containers well watered but not soggy. Bottom watering is best as it will not dislodge young seedlings and their tiny roots. Start fertilizing weekly with a weak solution (quarter-strength) of soluble fertilizer such as fish emulsion or manure tea.

About one week before the outdoor planting date, start moving the plants outside during the day and returning them indoors at night to "harden off" the seedlings and get them used to the outdoor environment.

While many seeds can be started outdoors in the beds and borders where they are to grow, still others actually benefit from direct sowing because they do not like to be transplanted. When starting seeds outdoors, the soil should be prepared first, and the seeds sown according to package directions. Annuals are sown

*Flats are placed outdoors during the day just prior to planting to "harden off" the seedlings.*

*Some seeds, like peas, are large enough to direct-sow by hand.*

© Derek Fell

## Seeds Requiring Special Attention

■ **Seeds that need light to germinate:** ageratum, balloon flower, basket of gold, beefsteak tomatoes, begonia, bellflower, blanket flower, browallia, coleus, columbine, coreopsis, creeping zinnia, dill, doronicum, flowering tobacco, fuchsia, gerbera, impatiens, lettuce, Mexican sunflower, ornamental cabbage, ornamental pepper, petunia, poppy (Oriental), most primrose, Queen-Anne's-lace, rock cress, red-flowered salvia, savory, Shasta daisy, snapdragon, stock, strawflower, sweet alyssum, and yarrow.

■ **Seeds that need darkness to germinate:** bachelor's button, borage, calendula, coriander, delphinium, fennel, forget-me-not, gazania, larkspur, nasturtium, pansy, poppy (except Oriental), phlox, sweet pea, verbena, vinca (annual), and viola.

anytime between early spring and the last spring frost, depending on the plant; perennials are sown anytime up to two months before the first autumn frost. After sowing seeds, firm the soil around them with your fingers. Seed beds must be kept constantly moist until the seeds have germinated. Once the seeds are growing and have developed two sets of leaves, they should be thinned to the spacing guidelines outlined on the seed packet or according to the directions given in the coming chapters. Thinnings can be transplanted to another part of the garden or shared with fellow gardeners.

## ■ GROWING PLANTS FROM CUTTINGS

Some annual flowers and herbs and many perennial flowers and herbs can be grown from stem cuttings instead of or in addition to seeds. To root a stem cutting, cut a piece of stem that contains at least four but preferably six to eight leaves. Remove the lower two leaves, and insert the leafless section of the stem into a container with premoistened soil-less medium. The same type of medium used for sowing seeds can be used for root cuttings. Applying rooting hormone to the bottom tip of the cutting will aid in and speed up rooting.

*Seeds of the popular snapdragon need light to germinate.*

- Seeds that require soaking or nicking before sowing: asparagus, baptisia, canna, hibiscus, lupine, morning glory, okra, parsley, parsnip, and sweet pea.

- Seeds that benefit from chilling before sowing: angelica, bleeding heart, columbine, daylily, gas plant, globe flower, lavender, lobelia (perennial), ornamental cabbage, pansy, phlox (perennial), primrose, trillium, and viola.

- Seeds that need cool temperatures (55°F, 13°C) to germinate: baby blue eyes, beard tongue, California poppy, candytuft (perennial), chamomile, coral bells, gas plant, phlox (annual), poppy, rosemary, sweet pea, thyme, and wallflower.

After the cutting is in place, put the container into a clear plastic bag and set it in a warm spot with good light but not direct sun. Test the cutting for rooting after several weeks by gently tugging on the stem. If it offers resistance, roots have formed, and the plastic bag can be removed. If the stem moves freely, rooting has not yet occurred. Return the cutting to the plastic bag, and try again after several weeks.

Once the cutting is rooted, it can be planted in the garden provided that the weather is cooperating at the time.

## ■ GROWING PLANTS FROM DIVISIONS

Many perennial plants can be increased by division, a practice that keeps them healthier and more floriferous or productive. To do this, dig them up from their beds in early autumn or when growth starts in early spring. Wash the soil off the roots, and pull the plants apart where they naturally and easily separate. If the roots are tightly woven together, you may need the help of a spading fork. Some root clumps will not split into sections easily, and these can be cut apart with a knife or spade. After dividing, replant the sections and water well.

*It's hard to resist the temptation of colorful plants when you visit a garden center in spring.*

## ■ BUYING PLANTS

In the spring, it's fun to visit local garden shops to purchase bedding plants of annual flowers, vegetables, and herbs instead of growing your own from seed, a method preferred by gardeners who lack either the time or the space to grow seedlings. Plants of perennial flowers and herbs are often sold at the same shops, or they may be purchased from a large number of mail-order nurseries. If you buy plants locally, look for deep green, healthy plants that are free of insects and diseases and neither too compact nor too spindly. Although it is tempting to select flowering annuals that are in bloom, it is better if they are not (except for most African marigolds, which must be in bud or bloom when planted or they will not bloom until late summer). Most annual flowers will come into full bloom faster in the garden if they are not in bloom when planted.

Most bedding plants are grown in individual "cell packs," although they may be in flats or individual pots. If it's not possible for you to plant them right away,

keep them in a lightly shaded spot and be sure to water them as needed, which will probably be every day. Just prior to planting, bedding plants should be well watered, as should the soil in the bed or border.

## ■ PLANTING

Before you plant your garden, it is a good idea to lay the plan of your beds and borders out on paper. The easiest way to do this is with graph paper. This will allow you to decide the shape and size of the borders and beds in advance. In addition, you will also know how many plants you will need to grow or buy. You can transfer the plan from the paper to the garden by laying it out with sticks and string.

Do not jump the gun on planting time! Tender annuals cannot be planted until after all danger of frost has passed and the soil is warm. Half-hardy annuals can be safely planted if nights are still cool as long as there will be no more frost. Hardy annuals can be planted in early spring as soon as the soil can be worked. Some

*Wait until the danger of frost has passed to add petunias and fountain grass to the flower bed or border.*

vegetables prefer cool weather, while others need warm temperatures. Naturally, their planting dates will vary. Perennial flowers and herbs can usually be planted as soon as the ground can be worked in spring, although some need autumn planting. Specific dates are outlined in the chapters on flowers, vegetables, and herbs.

When planting time comes, use the spacing guidelines outlined in the plant chapters. Lift plants from the container carefully, keeping the root ball intact to avoid damage. The best way to do this is to either gently squeeze or push up the bottom of the container if it is pliable enough or turn the container upside down and let the plant fall into your hand. If the plant does not slide out easily, tap the bottom of the container with a trowel. If the root ball is moist, as it should be, it should slip out easily without being disturbed.

Occasionally, plants are grown in containers that do not have individual cells. Separate the plants gently by hand or with a knife just prior to planting them so the roots do not dry out. Sometimes plants are grown in individual peat pots. To plant these, peel away a layer on the outside of the pot and put the plant and the pot into the ground. Be sure the top of the pot is below the soil level after planting or it will act as a wick and draw water away from the plants' roots. Any other type of container should be completely removed before planting.

If roots are extremely compacted, loosen them gently before planting so the plants will grow better. Dig a hole slightly larger than the root ball, set the plant in place at the same level it was growing in its container, and carefully fill in and firm up the soil around the roots. At all times, handle the plants by the root ball or the leaves, never by the stem, so as not to damage them. Water well after planting and again frequently until plants are established and new growth has started.

© Derek Fell

If possible, it is best to plant on a cloudy or overcast day or late in the afternoon to reduce transplanting shock. Petunias are the most notable exception to this rule, tolerating planting even on hot and sunny days.

## ■ WATERING

Deep, infrequent watering is better than frequent, light applications of water as the former encourages deep root growth, which results in healthier plants (refer to the individual plant descriptions in the chapters on flowers, vegetables, and herbs). When dry soil is called for, allow the top inch of soil to become dry before rewatering. When moist soil is required, never let the soil surface dry out. Plants with average water requirements can be watered when the soil surface becomes dry.

Unless it is very hot or windy, a weekly watering that applies one inch of water (if there is not one inch of rain) will usually suffice for plants with average water requirements. There's nothing you can do about the heat, but a fence or hedge can block the wind, preventing plants from drying out and lessening watering needs. Adjust watering for other plants that like drier or moister soil. One of the advantages of a highly organic soil is water retention, which will allow you to water less often and get your plants through dry periods better.

If possible, do not let the foliage become wet during watering, because this can spread disease. Soaker hoses, drip irrigation, or other methods of ground watering are the best way to achieve this. Vegetable gardens can be watered by digging furrows between the beds and filling the furrow with water. If overhead sprinklers must be used, however, you should water plants as early as possible in the day so that the foliage will dry out before night. When growing plants for cut flowers, do not water them overhead as this will cause water damage to the blooms. Hand watering is time-consuming except in very small gardens, but may be necessary for seedlings, containers, or where water-conservation practices are in force.

Where rainfall is low and water supplies are short, choose a drought-resistant plant, add additional organic matter to the soil, and mulch heavily with an organic mulch (see next section).

*Hand watering (LEFT) is more time consuming than other methods but gives you an excellent opportunity to evaluate how your garden is growing.*

*A wood-chip mulch (BELOW) is attractive and long lasting.*

## ■ MULCHING

A mulch is a layer of loose material that is placed on top of the soil. After your garden is planted, adding a 2- to 3-inch (5cm to 7.5cm) layer of mulch will not only add a note of attractiveness, it will also reduce the number of weeds, conserve soil moisture, keep the soil evenly moist, insulate the soil from temperature fluctuations, reduce soil erosion, and prevent disease organisms from splashing on the foliage. All of these result in better growth. The following year, the mulch can be incorporated into the soil before planting, enriching it with organic matter. Additional mulch can be added each spring, resulting in better soil structure and therefore better growth as years pass. In addition, most organic mulches have some nutrient value.

Peat moss should never be used as a mulch, because it actually draws water away from the soil, and once it is dry, it forms a crust that is very hard to remoisten. Which mulch you choose depends on your personal taste, availability, and cost.

## *Common natural mulches*

- **Bagasse (sugarcane)**—high water retention
- **Bark, chips or shredded**—good weed control
- **Buckwheat hulls**—attractive dark color
- **Cocoa bean hulls**—high in potassium (1–1–2.75)
- **Compost**—decomposes rapidly
- **Cottonseed hulls**—high in potassium and phosphorus (0–15–7)
- **Grass clippings**—dry first
- **Hay and straw**—may contain weed seeds
- **Leaf mold**—decomposes rapidly
- **Peanut hulls**—high in nitrogen (3.6–0.7–0.45)
- **Pine needles**—slow to decompose
- **Sawdust**—add extra nitrogen fertilizer
- **Wood chips**—slow to decompose

© Derek Fell

*Young tomatoes are
ready to climb the stakes,
protected by a mulch of
sheet plastic.*

© Jerry Pavia

## ■ WEEDING

A weed is simply a plant out of place. Weeding, however, is more than removing unwanted plants that make beds and borders unattractive. Weeds compete with plants for water, light, and nutrients, and they are breeding grounds for insects and diseases. Weeds are bound to appear even if you use mulch. Keep your eye out for them, and be sure to remove them as soon as possible. Try to remove weeds carefully, especially around young plants because you don't want to disturb their roots. They can be pulled by hand, or after the plants in your beds have matured, you can do your weeding with a hoe. Those that poke through mulch can easily be removed by hand.

Plants that require cool soil should be mulched immediately after planting, because this will keep the soil cool into the summer. Plants that like a hot climate and warm soil should not be mulched until the weather and the soil has warmed up. See the individual plant chapters for guidance on climate preference for flowers, vegetables, and herbs.

To reduce garden maintenance, especially weed pulling, choose a black plastic mulch, which also keeps the soil warm. Be sure to punch numerous holes into the plastic to ensure adequate water penetration into the soil below. A thin layer of decorative mulch will hide the plastic and add an attractive finishing touch to the garden. However, black plastic is not as beneficial to the soil as organic mulch. One option is to use it as a supplement to control weeds and apply it over the organic mulch, which will take advantage of the benefits of both.

© Susanna Pashko/Envision

## ■ STAKING AND TYING

Most flowering annuals and perennials do not need to
be staked, but now and then a few will grow too heavy
or too tall to stand up by themselves. Many vegetables,
especially vine crops, need staking, as do some herbs.
Use a sturdy stake of wood, plastic, or bamboo, and tie
the plant to it loosely with a twist-tie or string so it
won't be pinched or damaged. Setting the stake at
planting time will prevent damage to the roots. Large,
bushy plants may need three or four stakes around the
outside of the plant to keep them upright and compact.
Large plants can also be staked with tomato cages or
similar devices. Vining vegetables like beans can be
supported on trellises, A-frames, or tepees.

Some vines will cling on their own, but others
need help. Vines also need to be tied loosely to their
support to prevent damage to the stem. They can also
be woven through trellises and fences made of chicken
wire or similar material.

## ■ PINCHING AND PRUNING

A few annuals, primarily petunias, snapdragons, and
pansies, may need to be pinched back after planting or
after the first flush of bloom to keep them compact and
freely flowering. As new and more compact hybrids are
created, this is becoming less of a maintenance requirement. Sweet alyssum, basket of gold, candytuft, phlox,
and lobelia may tend to sprawl and encroach on walks,

*Tepees of poles are waiting
to be clothed in beans.*

Phlox subulata *(LEFT)*
*graces these steps but can be*
*trimmed back if it*
*encroaches too far.*

*Tender woody plants*
*(RIGHT) can be protected*
*in winter with a wire*
*cage filled with leaves.*

the lawn, or other flowers. They can be headed back with hedge clippers if this occurs. This shearing will also encourage heavier blooming. Pinching out the growing tips of perennial flowers early in the growing season will make the plants more compact and bushy and increase flowering. When flowers are cut from annuals or perennials for use in arrangements or because they have faded, the plants are in effect being pruned.

## ■ DEAD-HEADING

Some annual flowers, chiefly ageratum, begonias, coleus, impatiens, lobelia, salvia, sweet alyssum, and vinca, require little additional care. Their flowers fall cleanly from the plant after fading and do not need to be manually removed. Others, such as calendula, dahlias, geraniums, marigolds, and zinnias will need to have faded flowers removed. Most perennial flowers also need to have their faded flowers removed. This is known as dead-heading and prevents the plants from going to seed, wards off disease, and is necessary to keep them attractive and in full bloom. Dead-heading can be done with pruning shears or sometimes with the fingers.

## ■ AUTUMN CARE

In autumn, after frost has blackened the tops of flowers, vegetables, and herbs, the plants should be removed so the beds are not unsightly through the winter. Removal of plants also eliminates sites where insects and diseases can overwinter.

Winter protection may be necessary for some perennials. Refer to the zone map on page 186 to determine the hardiness zone of your garden. Then match this to the hardiness zones outlined in the chapter on flowers. If the hardiness of the plants you are growing falls below your hardiness zone, you will

need to apply winter protection. Winter protection also keeps perennials from being heaved from the soil during winter thaws.

Suitable materials for winter protection are shredded oak leaves, straw, and evergreen limbs from discarded Christmas trees. Apply winter protection several inches thick after the ground has frozen, and gradually remove it in spring as the weather warms. The mulch can be completely removed or worked into the soil to enrich and improve it.

## ■ COLD FRAMES AND HOT BEDS

A cold frame is a bottomless box with an adjustable transparent cover or lid made of glass, fiberglass, or plastic. Essentially, a cold frame is a type of miniature greenhouse. During the day, the cover or lid is left open and heat from the sun is trapped inside; at night, after the cover or lid is put in place, the air inside the cold frame stays warmer than the outside air.

© Derek Fell

*Gardening in containers (OPPOSITE) allows you to add accents throughout the yard.*

*Welcome spring with tulips and hyacinths (RIGHT).*

Cold frames can be used to protect plants from frost or to grow plants when the outside temperature is too cold. They can be used for starting seeds, growing seedlings, rooting cuttings, overwintering tender plants, or even growing a crop.

A hot bed is essentially the same thing as a cold frame, except that a hot frame has heating cables installed in the soil to provide additional heat.

## ■ GROWING PLANTS IN CONTAINERS

Growing plants in containers allows you to have flowers, vegetables, and herbs without a garden, often high above city streets. It is also a good way to add decorative accents to the garden.

Growing plants in containers requires more maintenance than caring for the same plants in the ground, but the ability to bring color into the landscape without planting beds makes it worth the effort. It also enables you to grow vegetables when you don't have space for a vegetable garden. The container can be made of wood, stone, ceramic, plastic, or anything that will hold planting medium and plants as long as it has adequate drainage. Keep in mind that metal containers may get too hot in the sun. You can use your imagination and plant container gardens into discarded tires, old shoes, bird cages, boxes, wheelbarrows, or tree stumps.

If the container does not have drainage holes and none can be made, a thick layer of gravel must be placed in the bottom of the planter to prevent waterlogging of the roots.

Garden soil should not be used in container plantings; it is too heavy, will not drain properly, and can introduce insects and diseases. This is a time when organic medium is essential. Mix or purchase a soil-less medium of peat moss or bark with perlite and/or

© Charles Mann

vermiculite. Fill the container to about $^1/_2$ inch (1.25cm) from the top before planting and water well. Space flowers closer than you would space them in the ground for a fuller effect.

Containers will need to be watered more than beds and borders because the growing area is limited and more prone to drying out, especially if the containers are in the sun or the wind. It is quite possible that daily watering may be necessary, so make sure a garden hose is accessible. Containers should also be fertilized lightly but frequently with a soluble plant food. If light strikes the planter unevenly, the growth of the plants in the container will be uneven. Rotate the container frequently to avoid this problem. Keep in mind that large containers are easier to move if they are placed on wheels or casters.

# Natural Insect and Disease Control

© Charles Mann

Whether we like it or not, nature has a way of interfering with our desire to grow perfect plants. Choosing insect- and disease-resistant varieties, providing plants with a rich, fertile soil so that they will grow strong, keeping plants well watered, and practicing good garden hygiene are all important steps to a healthy garden. But even the best-kept, well-maintained gardens are not invincible. Inevitably, some insects and diseases are bound to attack.

Fortunately, it is possible to naturally prevent or cure many of the ills that can beset a garden. These methods are slower and less complete than chemical methods, but the natural gardener realizes that nature's method of "integrated pest management" is effective and safer in the long run. It can take several years to build up a garden to the point where insects and diseases are controlled effectively, but the soil and the air will not be contaminated with chemicals.

*Disease-resistant vegetables (LEFT) are less susceptible to fungal, viral, and bacterial diseases.*

*Check seed packets (BELOW) for information on disease-resistant varieties of vegetables.*

Natural gardeners do not get upset at the appearance of a small infestation of insects. It is believed that 25 to 30 percent of the foliage can be stripped from a vegetable plant without loss of crop production. The ornamental gardener, however, would be hard pressed to tolerate this and would take steps to eradicate any problem. This chapter outlines ways to keep problems from arising and shows you how to solve any that do.

### ■ CONTROLLING DISEASES WITH GOOD GARDENING PRACTICES

Unfortunately, plants can become sick with diseases just as the gardeners who tend them can. When a plant becomes diseased, it is imperative that every attempt be made to cure it and prevent the spread of the disease to other plants. Remember that it is almost always easier to prevent a disease from occurring than it is to cure it once it's taken hold. Because well-maintained plants are less likely to succumb to diseases than weak ones, you can help ensure your plants' health by caring for them properly.

Plants are susceptible to a variety of fungal, viral, and bacterial diseases, whose effects can range from disfigurement to outright plant death. To reduce diseases in the garden, you may wish to plant only disease-resistant varieties, where they are available. Check seed packets or catalogs for this information. For example, there are disease-resistant varieties of asparagus, beans, beets, cabbage (and some of its relatives), celery, corn, cucumber, eggplant, lettuce, melons, onions, parsley, parsnips, peas, peppers, potatoes, sweet potatoes, and tomatoes. Check with the horticulture department of your cooperative extension office for the best disease-resistant varieties for your area.

Apart from practicing good garden hygiene and choosing disease-resistant plants, the best way to keep your plants from contracting diseases is to limit their exposure to the agents that spread them. Diseases are spread by insects, by direct contact with diseased plant material, and through the air, water, and soil. While you cannot shut your plants off from these influences completely, you can at least exert some control over them.

Where diseases are carried by insects, control of the pests will lessen or eliminate the disease. Watering your garden by drip irrigation rather than by overhead watering can help control some fungal diseases, which grow quickly under moist conditions. If you must water from above, do so in the morning to give leaves

*Japanese beetles (BELOW) are known to carry disease and should be removed with natural sprays, picked from plants by hand, trapped, or knocked off with a jet of water.*

and flowers a chance to dry by nightfall. Mulch will prevent water from splashing onto plants during rain or irrigation, contaminating them with disease spores from the ground. In some cases, adjusting the soil pH will reduce disease.

Good air circulation can also hold back mildew and other diseases by keeping plants dry and by not allowing disease spores to take hold. To enhance air circulation, do not set plants too close together, and do not let them grow into each other if they become large.

Weeds can harbor many diseases, such as blackspot and mildew, as well as disease-carrying insects such as Japanese beetles and leafhoppers. You can eliminate this potential breeding ground by keeping weeds in check. If your garden has a large number of weeds, use a mulch and hand weeding to control them. Insects known to be disease carriers can be eradicated with natural sprays or, if practical, picked from plants by hand, trapped, or knocked off with a jet of water.

© Anita Sabarese

To keep diseases from spreading in your garden by direct contact, prune away and destroy diseased parts of plants, and pick up diseased leaves as soon as they fall.

Some disease organisms, such as crown gall, are soilborne. Many have no means of prevention or cure, so when a plant becomes infected, the only remedy is to replace both it and the surrounding soil.

After working with diseased plants, wash your hands with soap and water to prevent the spread of disease, and wash all tools and rinse them with a 10 percent bleach solution to achieve the same effect.

## ■ CONTROLLING INSECTS AND OTHER PESTS WITH GOOD GARDENING PRACTICES

Hundreds of kinds of insects live in a typical garden, but only a handful of these regularly cause damage to plants. Indeed, some, such as lady beetles, are beneficial, because they consume harmful insects. Although the variety of attackers is small, the damage they do can be extensive. Left unchecked in a garden, insects can chew holes in leaves and flowers, suck vital juices from plants, spread diseases, and even kill the plants outright. Insect control is therefore essential to a healthy, productive garden.

Insects often live and lay eggs in weeds, so it is vital to keep the garden free of these breeding sites. Cleaning up garden debris as it accumulates and destroying it each autumn so that insects and their eggs cannot overwinter will also reduce the insect threat. Even the tidiest garden can harbor destructive insects, so it is wise to keep an eye out for early signs of infestation. Catching a problem early can save your garden from serious damage.

Specific vegetable varieties are available that are resistant to insect attack. These include varieties of

*Lady beetles (BELOW) are beneficial in the garden because they consume harmful insects.*

beans, cabbage and many of its relatives, corn, cucumbers, lettuce, melons, pumpkins, radishes, squash, sweet potatoes, and tomatoes. Check with the horticulture department of your cooperative extension office for the best insect-resistant varieties for your area.

It may be possible to delay the planting of certain crops until the insect no longer threatens. Keep records as to when insects appear in the garden, and postpone the planting date until after that if the growing season is long enough. You can also check with your county extension agent to get this information.

If you have an insect problem and you have been able to identify the species, you may choose to fight back with natural insecticides. Some insects, such as aphids, can be dislodged from the plants by a jet of water, but the application of insecticides is almost always a necessity at one time or another. Some of these insecticides, such as insecticidal soaps and pyrethrin sprays, are biological in origin, and these are the pesticides of choice for the natural gardener. See the section later in this chapter about identifying and controlling specific insects.

© Anita Sabarese

*Parasitic wasps will soon put an end to the destructive damage of this tomato hornworm.*

© Derek Fell

## ■ CROP ROTATION

Crop rotation has two main benefits. First, it keeps the soil at its most fertile level by rotating heavy feeders with light feeders and with legumes that fix nitrogen into the soil (see chapter six). Secondly, it inhibits the spread of insects and diseases, particularly soilborne diseases.

The principle behind crop rotation is to not plant the same plant or one of its close relatives in the same spot in succeeding years (a three- to six-year gap is recommended), because they would be prone to the same insect and disease problems. By introducing a different group of plants into a different section of the

garden each year, insects and diseases are kept to a minimum because their host plants are removed.

The following groups of plants should be grown and rotated together and should not follow each other in the same spot in the garden.

- eggplant, nicotiana, peppers, petunias, potatoes, tomatoes
- chives, garlic, leeks, onions, shallots
- beets, spinach, Swiss chard
- perennial alyssum, bok choy, broccoli, brussels sprouts, cabbage, cauliflower, collards, cress, kale, kohlrabi, mustard, radishes, rutabaga, turnip
- beans, lupines, peanuts, peas
- cucumbers, melons, pumpkins, squash
- chicory, endive, lettuce, marigolds, sunflowers, salsify
- corn, grains
- China aster, marigolds
- carrots, celeriac, celery, chervil, dill, parsley

## ■ NATURAL INSECT PREDATORS

Some gardeners prefer not to use sprays in their gardens, even natural ones, and instead rely on natural predators to control destructive insects. These helpful species include lady beetles (sometimes called ladybird beetles or ladybugs), assassin bugs, spined soldier bugs, green lacewings, praying mantids, parasitic wasps, predatory mites, and predatory nematodes. Lady beetles go after aphids, mealybugs, scales, and spider mites, while assassin bugs devour aphids, leafhoppers, small caterpillars, thrips, and spider mites. Spined soldier bugs feed on Mexican bean beetles and many caterpillars.

*A praying mantis preys on a drone fly; the mantis' legs have rows of sharp teeth to capture and hold its victim.*

© Anita Sabarese

Lacewings prefer a diet of aphids, mealybugs, scales, whiteflies, and spider mites, while praying mantids stick mainly to aphids. Braconid wasps diet on aphids, scales, many caterpillars, and some flies; one species feeds on leafrollers and another on cabbageworm. Trichogramma wasps destroy the eggs of almost all caterpillars. Predatory mites can control destructive mites. Parasitic nematodes feed on soil insects, including borers, cutworms, grubs, root maggots, and wireworms.

The drawback to introducing these insects is that once they have eaten the pests in your garden, they will move on to your neighbors' yards in search of additional food. As a result, their effectiveness may not be long-lived. You can purchase many of these insects by mail order; however, there are also some naturally occurring predatory insects that cannot be purchased, including ground beetles, spiders, and other types of wasps and flies.

77

## ■ COMPANION PLANTS

There are a number of plants known as companion plants that naturally repel insects. Some companion plants work on the entire garden whereas others work only in combination with specific plants. Why this happens is not completely understood by horticulturists, but for the natural gardener, the plain fact that it works is enough. While these companion plants are not entirely foolproof, they do have some merit and should be tried. They may not all work for you, but you can experiment to find other combinations that will. The basic premise is to interplant susceptible plants with other plants that either discourage or at least do not attract insects and diseases.

When planting companion plants, set the plants next to each other or in between each other in the same row or in zigzagged rows. In other words, plant them as close as possible.

The following chart lists the most successful companion plantings.

| PLANT | REPELS |
|---|---|
| Anise | Aphids, cabbage worm |
| Asparagus | Nematodes |
| Beans, castor | Gophers, moles |
| Beans, green | Colorado potato beetle |
| Borage | Tomato hornworm |
| Calendula | Nematodes |
| Catnip | Cabbage moth, Colorado potato beetle, cucumber beetle, flea beetle, squash bug |
| Celery | Cabbage moth |
| Chives | Aphids, mites, rabbits |
| Coriander | Aphids, Colorado potato beetle |
| Dahlia | Nematodes |
| Dill | Tomato hornworm |
| Flax | Colorado potato beetle |
| Garlic | Aphids, borers, gophers, Japanese beetle, mites, rabbits |
| Geranium | Leafhopper |

*Many believe that garlic has medicinal values; in the garden, it repels a number of insects and animals to keep plants healthy too.*

| PLANT | REPELS |
|---|---|
| **Horseradish** | Colorado potato beetle |
| **Marigold** | Aphids, Colorado potato beetle, nematodes, Mexican bean beetle, tomato hornworm, whitefly |
| **Mint** | Cabbage maggot, cabbage moth, flea beetles, mice |
| **Mustard** | Aphids on cole crops |
| **Nasturtium** | Cabbage moth, Colorado potato beetle, squash bug, whitefly |
| **Onion** | Borers, mites, rabbits |
| **Pennyroyal** | Ants, aphids |
| **Petunia** | Leafhopper, Mexican bean beetle |
| **Potato** | Mexican bean beetle |
| **Radish** | Cucumber beetle |
| **Rosemary** | Cabbage maggot, Mexican bean beetle |
| **Rue** | Japanese beetle |

| PLANT | REPELS |
|---|---|
| **Sage** | Cabbage maggot, cabbage moth |
| **Salvia (annual)** | Nematodes |
| **Soy beans** | Chinch bug |
| **Spearmint** | Ants, aphids |
| **Southernwood** | Ants, aphids, cabbage moth, flea beetles |
| **Summer savory** | Mexican bean beetle |
| **Tansy** | Ants, aphids, borers, Colorado potato beetle, cucumber beetle, cutworm, Japanese beetle, squash bug |
| **Thyme** | Cabbage moth |
| **Tomato** | Asparagus beetle, cabbage maggot, flea beetle on cole crops |
| **Wormwood** | Cabbage moth, flea beetle on cole crops, slugs and snails |

© Jerry Pavia

*Grow pretty rosemary plants for culinary uses as well as to repel cabbage maggots and Mexican bean beetles.*

*Traps baited with scents can be effective in controlling Japanese beetles.*

## ■ TRAP PLANTS

The idea behind this concept is to set "trap" plants in the garden that will lure pests away from other plants you want to keep pest-free. When insects appear on the trap plants, they should still be eradicated or controlled, but since the insects prefer the trap plants, your other plants will be bothered very little.

As examples, fruitworms prefer corn to tomatoes, so plant corn that you never intend to harvest to keep the tomatoes free of this pest. Summer squash protects winter squash from squash vine borers. Dill and borage attract the tomato hornworm, which will save the tomato plants from attack. Japanese beetles can be lured away from valuable crops with white or pastel zinnias and roses, odorless marigolds, and soybeans. Mustard will help keep harlequin bugs from cabbage, and green beans will be preferred by the Mexican bean beetle over soybeans.

## ■ TRAPS

Several types of insects can be trapped by mechanical devices. While this method is not completely effective, it helps some, especially in the early stages of infestation. It is also useful as a monitoring device to detect insect infestations in their early stages.

Whiteflies, tarnished plant bugs, aphids, and thrips are attracted to "sticky cards." These are yellow in color and covered with a sticky substance to which the insect adheres and cannot escape. You can buy sticky traps, or make your own with yellow cardboard, plastic, or wood covered with honey, molasses, 90-weight motor oil, or commercial products sold for this purpose.

Japanese beetles can be lured into traps baited with a pheromone (a sex hormone) that lures males. Some are also baited with floral scents to lure females. While

© Derek Fell

there is some controversy that these traps actually lure beetles from the area surrounding your garden, increasing your insect population, they may be of some benefit to you. Set them out in late spring just before beetles emerge, preferably in the sun.

Another way of trapping some insects is to place shallow yellow dishes (such as plastic margarine containers) filled with water on the ground. Some insects will fly into them and drown.

## ■ NATURAL PRODUCTS FOR INSECT AND DISEASE CONTROL

The following is an outline of the various products used by the natural gardener to control insects and diseases when cultural practices and other methods described above are not sufficient. Read this information carefully to determine which product is best suited for your problem.

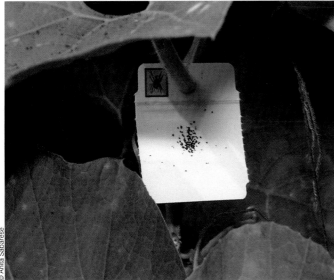

© Anita Sabarese

Insect traps can be useful to monitor insect infestations in the early stages.

## BT

*Bacillus thuringienses* is a biological control that is very effective against caterpillars, including the tomato hornworm and those caterpillars that feed on cole crops. There are several strains in addition to pure BT: BT San Jose controls Colorado potato beetles; BT kurstaki controls sod webworms; BT israelensis goes after mosquitoes. BT does not harm other pests, plants, honeybees, or animals. Since it works best on young caterpillars, apply it as soon as infestations appear.

## Copper sulfate

Copper sulfate is a fungicide and bactericide that is used chiefly against diseases of fruits and woody plants. However, when mixed with lime (8 ounces [240ml] of copper sulfate with 5 ounces [150ml] of lime in 6 gallons [22.8l] of water), it is known as Bordeaux mixture and is a good fungicide for ornamentals and edibles to combat anthracnose, leaf spot, and mildew.

## Diatomaceous earth

The dried, ground skeletons of microscopic algae, diatomaceous earth has sharp edges that puncture the outer parts of soft-bodied insects, causing them to die from loss of body fluids. It can be applied to wet foliage or to the ground to help control aphids, caterpillars, grubs, maggots, and other crawling insects.

*Insect traps can be useful to monitor insect infestations in the early stages.*

## Dormant oil

Dormant oil is a mineral oil used in early spring on dormant woody plants to control the eggs and sometimes the adults of aphids, leaf rollers, mites, and scales. While it is not a product for direct use on annuals, herbs, perennials, or vegetables, it can be used in early spring to control insects on woody plants that can later spread to all plants in the garden.

## Lime sulfur

Calcium polysulfide, known as lime sulfur, acts as both an insecticide and a fungicide/bactericide. It combats anthracnose, leaf spot, mildew, and rust and is effective against scales, thrips, and some mites. Do not use it if the temperature is over 85°F (30°C) as leaf burn could result.

## Milky spore disease

Milky spore disease is a biological control, either *Bacillus popilliae* or *B. lentimorbus*. When applied to the soil, it is effective against the grubs of Japanese beetles, Oriental beetles, some May and June beetles, and rose chafer. As the grubs feed on the spores, they die, releasing new spores that will kill future grubs. Milky spore disease can be effective for 15 to 20 years or more. It is usually applied to lawns but can be applied to flower and vegetable beds as well. Local cooperative extention offices can provide information on the effectiveness of this treatment in specific regions.

## Nicotine sulfate

This tobacco extract does not hold the same popularity as an insecticide as it once did. It works against aphids, asparagus beetles, leafhoppers, leaf miners, mealybugs, mites, scales, squash bugs, and thrips. The liquid concentrate is very toxic, however, so it cannot be used on

© John A. Lynch/Photo/Nats

*Cottony cushion scale (LEFT) is just one type of insect that can be controlled by using a soap solution.*

*Whiteflies have found a home on these lantana leaves (BELOW) but can be attracted away with yellow sticky cards.*

## Sabadilla

Sabadilla is an extract from the seeds of sabadilla, a lilylike plant. Its use is best directed after armyworms, blister beetles, cabbage loopers, cucumber beetles, harlequin bugs, leafhoppers, and squash bugs.

## Soap

Soap solutions are effective insecticides against many insects as the soap film smothers them. You can purchase insecticidal soap or make your own with 3 tablespoons (45ml) of soap flakes or 3 to 6 tablespoons (46 to 90ml) of liquid soap in a gallon of water. Be sure not to use detergents or caustic laundry soap. Soap solutions are effective in combating aphids, leafhoppers, mites, scales, and whiteflies on contact.

## Sulfur

Elemental sulfur in powdered form is a fungicide used to control botrytis, leaf spot, downy and powdery mildew, and scab. It also has insecticide effectiveness

tomatoes or their relatives for fear of spreading tobacco mosaic virus. There is a one-month waiting period between spraying and harvest for edible crops.

## Pyrethrum

Pyrethrum is an extract of a species of chrysanthemum that has quick-acting control over larger beetles and caterpillars. It can also control aphids, harlequin bugs, leafhoppers, some flies, and squash bugs. However, it is toxic to fish and can damage beneficial insects.

## Rotenone

Rotenone, an extract from the roots of some tropical legumes, is toxic primarily to chewing insects. It controls aphids, many types of beetles, carpenter ants, and some mites. It is toxic to fish and some beneficial insects.

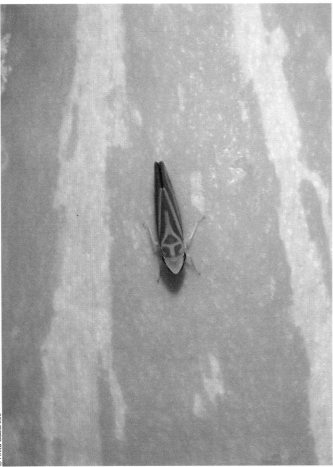

© Anita Sabarese

*Protect squash (LEFT)
from leaf hoppers with
weed control, netting, or
pyrethrum sprays.*

## ■ HOME REMEDIES

Many natural gardeners swear by home remedies, products you can easily make in your kitchen. While there is no scientific proof that these remedies work, they can do little or no harm and might just do the trick for you if you want to try them. Try spraying them on a few leaves first, and if no damage occurs to the plant in three days, the entire plant can be sprayed. These remedies include the following.

- Extract of tomato leaves to combat aphids
- Extract of garlic to control aphids, cabbage loopers, earwigs, June bugs, leafhoppers, squash bugs, and whiteflies
- Extract of garlic, onion, and cayenne pepper to control any leaf-chewing insects
- Herbal extracts: catnip, chives, feverfew, hyssop, marigolds, nasturtium, rosemary, rue, sage, tansy, thyme, or wormwood to control leaf-eating insects
- Dusts of hot peppers to repel root maggots

against aphids, leafhoppers, and spider mites. Whether used as a dust or spray, do not use if the temperature is over 85°F (30°C).

## *Summer oil*

Summer oil is similar to dormant oil but lighter. Therefore, it can be used when foliage is on the plants. Its use is recommended only for woody plants; it can be used, however, to check the spread of aphids, leafhoppers, mealybugs, mites, scales, and whiteflies to the flower, herb, or vegetable garden. Do not use unless the temperature will remain below 90°F (32°C) for 24 hours to prevent burn.

In addition to using these products, spreading bone meal, powdered charcoal, lime, or wood ashes on the ground around susceptible plants often controls maggots and ground insects.

## ■ DISEASES AND DISEASE CONTROL

In addition to cultural practices, diseases can be controlled with sprays known as fungicides. The most common natural fungicides are sulfur or products containing sulfur, such as lime sulfur and Bordeaux mixture. In general, preventive spraying in advance of the problem will give better results than waiting until the disease occurs and then trying to cure it.

Experimentation is being done on three products that show promise for disease control. One is baking soda, which when diluted at a rate of 1 teaspoon (5ml) per quart (.95l) of water has controlled scab. Another is a range of antidesiccants, which are applied to

evergreens in late autumn to prevent their drying out
over the winter. These have demonstrated some control
over powdery mildew and possibly other diseases.
Dormant oils, which are used in early spring to control
insects, may also have disease-fighting properties.
Remember that these controls are not proven, although
you may want to experiment with them.

Whatever product you decide to use, however,
proper diagnosis of a disease is necessary to initiate the
right control measures. If you have a problem you
cannot identify, your garden center, local gardening club,
or cooperative extension office will be able to help. Once
you know what you are dealing with, you will know
how to handle the problem. The following descriptions
of plant diseases will help you make your diagnosis.

## Anthracnose

■ **Symptoms:** Sunken black or purple spots appear on
foliage, vegetables, and fruit. Leaves turn black and
shrivel, especially in wet weather. Flowers may not
develop. Spots may also develop on stems.

■ **Control:** Buy varieties of vegetables with anthracnose
resistance, and rotate crops. Keep beans and peppers
separated, and don't touch bean plants when the foliage
is wet. Prune away any damaged plant parts and remove
fallen leaves from the garden. Spray with copper sulfate,
lime sulfur, or Bordeaux mixture.

## Aster yellows

■ **Symptoms:** Leaves suddenly turn yellow; flowers
are misformed and greenish in color. Annuals and
perennials are chiefly affected.

■ **Control:** Control leafhoppers, which spread the
disease. Remove and destroy infected plants; do not
use the same type of plant in the same spot the following year. Keep the garden well weeded. There are no
other controls.

## Botrytis blight

(also called gray mold)

■ **Symptoms:** Leaves and growing tips turn black.
Flower buds turn black and may not open; if they do,
the flowers may be streaked in brown and are covered
with a gray fuzzy growth.

*Good air circulation, avoiding wet leaves at night, rotating plants, and spraying with sulfur will control botrytis (BELOW) on geraniums and other plants.*

■ **Control:** Avoid watering at night and improve air circulation. Cut away any infected plant parts. Rotating crops will lessen botrytis attack. Spray with sulfur to prevent or control the disease.

## Damping off
■ **Symptoms:** Seeds rot before they germinate, or new seedlings suddenly fall over and die.
■ **Control:** Use sterile, soil-less medium that has not been used before for starting seeds. Be sure the growing medium has excellent drainage, and do not overwater. Do not overcrowd seedlings, either outdoors or indoors. Where damping off has been a problem outdoors, cover seeds after sowing with vermiculite instead of soil.

## Leaf spot
■ **Symptoms:** Spots appear on the upper and/or undersides of leaves; the spots may be black, brown, or purple and are often surrounded by yellow halos.
■ **Control:** Remove damaged leaves and spray with sulfur, lime sulfur, or Bordeaux mixture to prevent or control the disease. Water early in the day. Clean up

*Blackspot (BOTTOM) on roses, like other leafspots, can be controlled with good air circulation, ridding the garden of infected leaves, and spraying with sulfur compounds.*

and discard fallen leaves. Prune plants back, as disease spores live on the stems as well as on the leaves. Also look for resistant varieties.

## Mildew
(powdery and downy)
■ **Symptoms:** Powdery mildew is characterized by a white or gray dusty powder that coats leaves, stems, and flower buds. Downy mildew is characterized by gray or tan fuzzy growths on the undersides of the leaves. With both diseases, leaves and flowers become distorted, turn yellow, and fall.
■ **Control:** Remove and destroy infected leaves. Treat plants with a fungicide to prevent spread of the disease. Fungicides containing sulfur, such as elemental sulfur, lime sulfur, and Bordeaux mixture will control and may eliminate mildew. Improve air circulation, and water early in the day.

## Mosaic
■ **Symptoms:** Leaves become mottled or streaked with yellow or light green. Leaves may curl and plants are often stunted. Vegetables may be discolored or streaked.

*Wilt diseases (BELOW) are
soilborne and incurable;
prevention is the key to
avoiding them.*

© Derek Fell

■ **Control:** There are no spray controls for this virus
disease. Remove and discard severely infected plants.
Control aphids, which spread the disease, and keep the
garden weed free. Look also for resistant varieties.
Sometimes the symptoms disappear by themselves.

## Rust
■ **Symptoms:** Upper leaf surfaces turn pale; lower leaf
surfaces are covered with orange powder.
■ **Control:** Water early in the day. Remove infected
leaves and clean up any fallen leaves and stems. Spray
with lime sulfur to prevent or control the disease. Do not
work among rust-susceptible plants when the foliage is
wet. Some varieties of plants are rust resistant.

## Scab
■ **Symptoms:** Gray or black sunken spots or raised,
sometimes corky, growths appear mostly on fruits and
vegetables, although leaves may also show some
spotting.
■ **Control:** Remove and destroy infected fruit and
vegetables. Spray with sulfur to prevent and control
the disease.

## Wilt, fusarium wilt, verticillium wilt
■ **Symptoms:** Vegetable plants suddenly wilt and die.
Foliage of perennials and annuals turns yellow, then
brown, then wilts and drops. Symptoms first appear at
ground level and work their way up the plant.
■ **Control:** There are no cures for wilt diseases, which
are soilborne. Prune out any infected plant parts.
Totally diseased plants should be removed and
destroyed. Soil replacement is necessary in severe cases.
There are varieties of vegetables, perennials, and
annuals that are wilt-resistant. Rotate crops, and lower
the amount of nitrogen fertilizer applied.

## ■ INSECTS AND INSECT CONTROL
In addition to cultural controls, handpicking, and traps,
insects in the garden can be stopped with a number of
natural sprays known as insecticides. In almost all cases,
it is better to wait until you notice early signs of infestation to spray your plants, as preventive-spraying measures
rarely work in insect control and are costly as well.

Many insects are large enough to be seen, making
their identification easy. In other cases, where the
insects are tiny, the symptoms of their damage will
have to be studied to identify them. The following
descriptions of insects and their damage will help you
identify your problem and deal with it properly.

*A major potato pest, Colorado potato beetle (BELOW), also attacks other plants and can be controlled with mulch, companion plants, hand-picking, and natural sprays.*

In order for most natural insecticides to work, they must come into direct contact with the insect. Dormant oil and insecticidal soap are types of contact insecticides that kill insects by smothering them or their eggs with a film. So it is important to remember when spraying that you hit your target. The major exception to this is BT, which remains on plant leaves to kill the insect as it feeds.

Mites, snails, and slugs are technically not insects but are included in this section because the damage they do is similar to insect damage. Mites are related to spiders, and snails and slugs are molluscs.

Some natural sprays can also destroy natural predators and other beneficial insects, so organic gardeners often use them only as a last resort. Here is a list of common garden pests, the symptoms of infestation, and how to get them under control.

© Anita Sabarese

## Aphids

■ **Symptoms:** Small, semitransparent, green, black, brown, red, or yellow insects cluster on buds, leaves, and stems and suck plant juices. The leaves curl, wither, and may turn yellow, and a clear, shiny substance known as honeydew appears on the leaves. A black, sooty mold is sometimes present. Aphids also transmit plant diseases.

■ **Control:** Knock aphids off the plant with a strong stream of water. Spray woody plants with dormant oil in early spring, and spray all plants with insecticidal soap when insects appear. Aphids can be handpicked, controlled with predatory insects, or treated with diatomaceous earth, pyrethrum, rotenone, or sulfur. A mulch of aluminum foil around low-growing plants also wards off aphids.

## Beetles

■ **Symptoms:** Round holes appear in leaves and sometimes in the flowers, stems, or fruits. Insects with hard shells of varying colors, sometimes striped or spotted, are visible.

■ **Control:** Small infestations can be controlled by handpicking (always wear gloves when picking blister beetles). Rotenone is effective against asparagus, Colorado potato, cucumber, flea, Japanese, and Mexican bean beetles. Sabadilla can be used to fight blister and cucumber beetles, and pyrethrum will combat Mexican bean beetles. Milky spore disease destroys the grubs of some beetles. Traps catch Japanese beetles with limited effectiveness. Diatomaceous earth has some effect on flea beetles. A heavy mulch will keep Colorado potato beetles down. Small plants may be protected with a woven, mesh, or net covering. Keep the garden weed free, and try introducing predatory insects.

*Keep a watchful eye out for caterpillars (BELOW) and control with handpicking or natural sprays.*

## Bugs

(Although many refer to any insect as a "bug," there is a class of insect properly known as "bugs.")

■ **Symptoms:** Leaves and stems are chewed and may turn yellow and die; new growth turns black; flower buds die. Insects with crossed wings are visible.

■ **Control:** Handpick when possible. Sabadilla and pyrethrum control harlequin and tarnished plant bugs; sabadilla controls squash bugs; rotenone combats harlequin bugs. Sticky traps give some control of tarnished plant bug. Eliminate garden weeds.

## Caterpillars

(larvae of moths and butterflies)

■ **Symptoms:** Holes appear in leaves and sometimes the whole leaf is consumed. Buds, flowers, fruit, and stems may also be stripped from the plant. Long, thin insects of varying sizes and colors are visible.

■ **Control:** Most caterpillars can be handpicked and destroyed. All can be controlled with BT. Rotenone is

© Anita Sabarese

effective against cabbage loopers and cabbageworms; sabadilla against cabbage loopers and armyworms; and pyrethrum against cabbageworms. Diatomaceous earth has some effect against most caterpillars. Placing a protective collar around young seedlings will prevent cutworm damage. Placing summer oil on corn silks as they form will hold down the corn earthworm. Small plants can be covered with mesh, netting, or cheesecloth.

## Leafhoppers

■ **Symptoms:** Leaves turn yellow or are speckled with dots and eventually curl up and die. Leafhoppers are light green or gray, wedge-shaped insects that move quickly and are visible. They are a further problem because they spread disease.

■ **Control:** Remove damaged leaves and treat plants with insecticidal soap, pyrethrum, sabadilla, or sulfur. Diatomaceous earth also has some effect.

## Maggots

■ **Symptoms:** Plants fail to grow, turn yellow, and die. Inspection of the roots shows that they have been consumed by small, wormlike insects, the larvae of flies. Cabbage and its relatives and onion and its relatives are mostly affected.

■ **Control:** Sprinkle diatomaceous earth or wood ashes on the ground around plants. Cover young plants with cheesecloth. Place a protective collar around plants.

## Mealybugs

■ **Symptoms:** Growth is stunted, leaves turn yellow and wilt. White, cottony growth is visible on the stems and the undersides of leaves.

■ **Control:** Remove by hand, or dab insects with a cotton swab that has been dipped in alcohol. Spray with soap solution, and introduce predatory insects.

*Cottony tufts indicate a mealybug (BELOW) problem; these insects suck sap* *and life from a large number of plants.*

*Baited shallow dishes (BOTTOM) easily lure and kill slugs.*

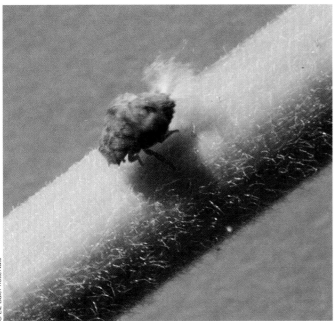

## Mites

- **Symptoms:** Leaves become speckled with yellow and take on a dull bronze sheen. The undersides of the leaves show small black, red, yellow, or green spots. Webbing becomes evident in advanced cases. Mites are technically not insects, but they do suck plant juices the way many insects do.
- **Control:** Mist the undersides of the leaves on a daily basis. Treat with soap solution, sulfur, or lime sulfur. Rotenone works on some mites. Introduce predatory insects and mites.

## Nematodes

- **Symptoms:** Plant suddenly loses color, wilts, and dies. Digging up the plant reveals swollen and knotted roots. Nematodes are wormlike animals and are not visible.
- **Control:** There are no effective spray treatments. In severe cases, remove plants and the surrounding soil, and replace. Large plantings of marigolds repel destructive nematodes. Plant resistant varieties of plants.

## Scale

- **Symptoms:** Plants stop growing and growing tips die back. Leaves turn yellow and fall from the plant. Clusters of insects are visible on stems and branches. The insects are round, oval, or crescent-shaped; some have a soft shell while others have a hard shell.
- **Control:** Prune out any dead or infested stems. Scrub scales off with a brush, and treat with soap solution or lime sulfur.

## Slugs and snails

- **Symptoms:** Holes appear in leaves; young plants may disappear completely. Silvery trails are visible on leaves and along the ground. Slugs and snails are mostly visible at night.

*Avoid attack by the squash vine borer (BELOW) by planting squash as late in the season as possible.*

*The telltale signs of squash-vine borers (BOTTOM) are sudden wilting and a yellow sawdustlike material around holes in the stems.*

■ **Control:** Trap in shallow saucers of beer, inverted grapefruit halves, or purchased traps. They can be handpicked and destroyed, although most people find it distasteful to handle slugs. They will shrivel when salt is poured on them, but salt is toxic to the soil and surrounding plants. Diatomaceous earth is effective, as are copper barriers set into the ground. Remove debris and eliminate cool, dark, damp daytime hiding places from your garden.

## Squash-vine borers

■ **Symptoms:** Foliage and stems of squash suddenly wilt; growth slows or stops. A caterpillarlike insect can be located within the stem.

© Derek Fell

■ **Control:** Cut back the stem until the borer is found, and discard it. Alter planting dates if possible until after the chance of attack is past. Bury every fifth leaf node on vining squash so the plant will root and keep growing if infested.

## Thrips

■ **Symptoms:** Leaves curl, and leaf margins turn white, yellow, or brown. Flower buds are discolored and may not open; if they do, the petals are streaked in brown. The insects are tiny flies and not visible.

■ **Control:** Remove and destroy infested plant parts. Treat with soap solution or lime sulfur. Several predatory insects are effective.

## Whiteflies

■ **Symptoms:** Small, white insects congregate on the undersides of leaves and fly in clouds when disturbed. Leaves are mottled in yellow and curl up, and may be covered in black sooty mold.

■ **Control:** Spray with soap solution. Trap with yellow sticky cards.

## ■ SPRAYERS

Although a few insecticides and fungicides are poured onto the ground or applied in dry form to it, most are applied directly to the plants' foliage as a spray. Ready-to-use products are available, but for larger gardens, it is more economical to purchase a sprayer and natural chemical concentrates to dilute yourself.

There are several different types of sprayers, all widely available at garden and hardware stores. A compression sprayer has a tank for the spray solution (usually holding 1½ to 2 gallons [5.7 to 7.6l]), a plunger to compress air into the container, and a piece of tubing with a nozzle at the end. It is pumped with air after the diluted material is mixed into it to build up pressure to deliver a spray from the handheld tank. Both metal and plastic types are available; plastic ones are lighter in weight and resist corrosion. Compression sprayers are the most convenient and popular type.

Some small sprayers are driven by rechargeable batteries that eliminate the need for hand pumping. Most will hold an overnight charge for 45 minutes—enough time to spray the average garden.

Other kinds of sprayers, called hose-end sprayers, are designed to be attached to the end of a garden hose. Most consist of a nozzle and a detachable plastic bottle that holds a concentrated solution of insecticide or fungicide. Water from the hose siphons and dilutes the concentrate and propels the mixture through the nozzle. This is the least convenient sprayer to use, since it requires you to drag a hose around—an inconvenience in a large or crowded garden. This type of sprayer may also distribute the concentrate unevenly. Proportioners of the type used to apply large amounts of liquid fertilizer can also be used to apply spray materials.

Some sprayers have long tubular or sliding attachments called trombones that make it easy to spray tall plants or vines. These trombone-action sprayers are pumps, not compression sprayers, and pump solution out of a bucket. Tank sprayers that roll on wheels are also available and are convenient for use in very large gardens; some of these have motorized compressors.

Garden centers also sell dusters for the application of powdered insecticides and fungicides; they are tubular devices with a plunger at one end. In recent years, however, they have given way to sprayers, since spraying a liquid is a more even and effective way to apply materials.

*If only a few plants need spraying, a small handheld sprayer (BELOW) can be very convenient.*

*For spraying large gardens (RIGHT), use economical concentrates mixed with water.*

## ■ APPLYING NATURAL SPRAYS

Once you have diagnosed your insect and disease problems, you can determine what spray material to use, either by consulting sections earlier in this chapter, asking at your local garden center, or consulting your county extension agent. Some of these products are sprayed directly onto the plants, while others are applied to the ground. Dormant sprays are applied to woody plants in early spring before the plants show signs of life; other formulations are applied throughout the growing season at intervals specified on their labels.

Natural spray materials are usually available wherever gardening supplies are sold and from mail-order firms specializing in natural gardening products. Most are concentrates that must be diluted with water before you use them. Some of these are liquids; others

are powders or granules that either dissolve or go into suspension in water. Several products come fully diluted and ready to use and are convenient if you have only a few plants. For large gardens, however, concentrates are much less expensive.

When working with concentrates, read the label carefully and dilute the substance exactly as directed. The label will also tell you how long you have to wait between application and harvesting of food crops.

Determine how much water you will need and add one quarter of it to the empty sprayer (hot water works best to dissolve dry materials). Then add the concentrate and mix it well by agitating the sprayer. Pour in the remaining water and mix again, making sure the ingredients are fully dissolved or suspended before spraying. The label will also tell you how often repeat treatment may be needed.

Fungicides are usually needed every seven to ten days throughout the growing season. Insect sprays should be applied as directed on the label; spraying should usually stop when there are no more signs of infestation. When applying insecticides, it is usually best to treat only the affected plants, not the entire garden. One exception to this rule is milky spore disease, because the entire garden must be treated for adequate control.

It is possible to mix different products together— for example, an insecticide and a fungicide—so that more than one treatment is applied at a time. Before mixing two products, however, make sure that both their labels recommend this; if the mixing directions seem too complicated, you may choose to apply the products separately. If you are combining a powder and a liquid, add the powder first to one quarter of the total water needed, and after it has dissolved or is suspended,

© Derek Fell

add the liquid before adding the rest of the water. Label instructions give dilution rates in units per gallon (or liter) of water. When combining products, dilute each one as if it were the only ingredient; do not increase the total amount of the water.

Always mix chemicals outdoors in a well-ventilated area, and do not eat, drink, or smoke while handling them. Remove your clothes and take a shower as soon as you have finished spraying. Never reuse a spray solution; mix only what you need for one application. If there is any left over, dispose of it properly and care-

fully. You can pour it into an empty bottle, seal it, wrap it in newspaper, and place it in the trash; or spray it on other plants listed on the product label. Always discard empty containers; never burn or incinerate them.

Do not buy more insecticides or fungicides than you will use in a year or two, because many products can lose their effectiveness over time. Always store products in the original container in a place where children will not be able to reach them; if possible, keep them under lock and key. Also keep them out of the sun and heat.

## ■ SPRAYING TIPS

Before you use a sprayer for the first time, be sure to read the instructions accompanying it. Sprayers differ in design and operation, so it is important to follow the instructions carefully. Here are some general pointers.

■ Make sure plants are well watered before you spray, since damage is more likely to occur to dry leaves than

to moist, turgid ones. Never spray on a windy day; too much of your spray will be blown away.

■ Spray both the upper and lower leaf surfaces until the spray starts to run off the leaf. Nozzles on some sprayers can be adjusted to produce different droplet sizes; the finer the spray, the more even the coverage.

■ When using a compression sprayer, you will need to

*Strawberries protected with netting (ABOVE) will mean more berries for the table and less for the birds.*

*Always water plants well (LEFT) before spraying to avoid spray damage.*

repump it once or twice during spraying to keep the pressure high enough to deliver a fine spray.

■ If the sprayer contains powdered material in suspension, you may need to shake it several times during spraying to keep the material evenly dispersed in the water. Adding a squirt of liquid soap to the water in the sprayer if powdered material is being used, either in suspension or in solution, will help it adhere better to the plants' leaves.

■ Keep your sprayer in good working order by cleaning and maintaining it properly. Nozzle apertures are small and clog easily; after each use, fill the sprayer with plain water, and spray it through the nozzle to flush out any residue. If the nozzle becomes clogged, clean it by poking a thin wire through it. If you have a compression sprayer, you may need to apply light oil to its pump cylinder from time to time to keep it working smoothly.

## ■ ATTRACTING BIRDS TO THE GARDEN

Many gardeners love to attract birds to the garden by providing the basic essentials of life for them: food, shelter, and water. Many birds, especially creepers, flycatchers, nuthatches, swallows, warblers, and woodpeckers, feed on insects and can help keep the insect population under control. Unfortunately, these critters do not discriminate when they feed and can eat beneficial as well as destructive insects.

Gardeners maintaining edible gardens often cringe when birds visit, because of the damage they do in getting to the crop first. Nylon mesh, fine woven material, or fine netting can be placed over vegetable

*Let your imagination run wild when building a scarecrow (LEFT) to keep birds away from your harvest.*

*Cover plants with a chicken-wire cage (BELOW) to keep rabbits from feasting on your garden.*

plants as well as small fruits and berries to protect them from birds. Scarecrows and other repelling devices can also keep birds away from food gardens.

## ■ RODENT AND ANIMAL CONTROL

Gardens, especially those in rural areas, can be menaced by a variety of animals and small rodents. Some of these devour destructive insects, but the harm they do to plants far outweighs their good. While there are no foolproof methods of controlling them, some measures will reduce their damage.

Squirrels, field mice, and chipmunks often dig up small plants. This can be reduced by laying a piece of chicken wire over the planting bed and securing it.

Many animals can be trapped and removed to another area, but they often return.

The odor of dried blood may repel some small animals. However, dried blood is ineffective after the first rain or watering. It also contains nitrogen, so you will need to recalculate your fertilizer needs if you use it often.

To keep rabbits out of a vegetable garden, surround the garden with a chicken-wire fence that is 2¹/₂ feet (75cm) high and extends 6 inches (15cm) under the ground. Watch for signs of rabbits burrowing under the fence, and repair if necessary. Rabbits can also be deterred with phosphate rock dusted around plants, blood meal, bonemeal, or cayenne pepper.

Deer can be deterred with an electric fence or with a fence built with an extension angled out 8 feet (2.4m) from it, which will keep deer from jumping it. Outside dogs may keep deer away as well.

Moles, voles, and gophers burrow under the ground, eating roots and pushing plants up. Gophers can be controlled with repellents or traps set in their

© Derek Fell

tunnels. Moles can be trapped, and tobacco, red pepper, or castor oil may deter them. If you see a tunnel, step on it right away, and push the plants back into the ground. Cats help control voles and field mice, which can also be trapped.

There are repellents you can purchase; read the label carefully to be sure they are made of natural products. You can make your own repellent by soaking strips of heavy material in creosote and hanging them around the garden. Some gardeners find that human hair is an effective repellent.

Avoid placing winter protection around perennials until after the ground has frozen to deter small animals from nesting under the mulch. Keeping the garden clear of debris will also help to discourage small animals.

Refer to the section on companion plants for suggestions of plants that deter animals and rodents.

# THE NATURAL FLOWER GARDEN

© Charles Mann

*One of the backbones of the perennial garden, phlox (ABOVE) enlivens the midsummer garden.*

*Allocating space for a garden bench (RIGHT) will not only enhance the flower garden, it will also allow you to enjoy it more.*

You are proud of your home and your garden. Tall trees provide shade and a strong framework; shrubbery enhances the areas near the house and line the path to the front door; outdoor living areas are comfortable, framed with a lush, green lawn. Yet, something seems to be missing. Color. Although flowering trees, shrubs, and bulbs enliven the garden, one of the most satisfying and diversified ways to bring color to the garden is with flowering annuals and perennials.

Whatever look you wish to achieve can be accomplished with annuals and perennials. No matter what the weather, location, or length of the growing season, there is a large selection of annuals and perennials to beautify the garden. From earliest spring when pansy and primrose faces pop up from flower beds, through the warmer summer months when marigolds, zinnias, iris, and phlox blaze with color, into the crisp

🌿 *100*

*Even small spaces (BELOW) can be turned into over-flowing color as in this country garden.*

*Grow plants in containers (RIGHT) if you don't have much room for a garden in the ground.*

days of autumn when chrysanthemums and ornamental kale or cabbage add new tones to fallen leaves, there are annuals and perennials to fit the bill.

Flowers can be used to define areas or to accent them, to unite large sections of the garden or to make the garden seem larger or smaller. The smallest of cottage gardens or balconies high over city streets benefit from containers of colorful flowers. Cut flowers can cheer up the indoors for many months. Perennials form the backbone of the flower garden, returning dependably year after year, whereas one of the nicest things about annuals is that by planting different varieties you can change the mood of your garden. Go hot one year with beds of red, yellow, and orange flowers, and be cool the following year with shades of blue, violet, white, and gray pastels.

While separate beds and/or borders can be allocated to annuals and perennials, a beautiful look is achieved when the two are interplanted. The everblooming characteristic of annuals will bring continuity to the planting during any period when the perennials may not be at their peak of bloom. Since most perennials bloom for only three to six weeks, it is possible that there will be a time, even with good plant selection, when the perennials will not offer much color, letting the annuals take over.

*When irises (RIGHT) stop blooming profusely, it's time to dig them up and divide them.*

*As soon as the flowers of Oriental poppies (OPPOSITE) have faded, clip them off.*

Technically, an annual is a plant that grows, flowers, sets seed, and dies in one growing season. Some tender perennials and biennials that will not survive cold winters but will grow and bloom in one growing season are also referred to and grown as annuals. A biennial is a plant that is set into the ground during the first growing season. After overwintering, it blooms the second year. While there are not a large number of biennials, the most common ones will be covered in this chapter. A perennial, as the name implies, dies to the ground after the first frost but grows and flowers again for at least two years.

Annuals are divided into three categories. Tender annuals are injured by frost and are not planted until all danger of frost has passed in spring and the ground is warm; they grow all summer until killed by the first frost of autumn. Half-hardy annuals, although they do not tolerate frost, will grow during cool weather and can be planted in mid-spring. Hardy annuals will withstand some frost and are planted in late autumn, late winter, or early spring for early color. In the plant descriptions that appear later, the hardiness of each annual is indicated. Use this as a guide for planting time.

Perennials can be planted anytime from mid-spring through autumn. Poppies, irises, and peonies must be planted in autumn or they will not bloom the first year. With both annuals and perennials, follow the spacing outlined in the plant dictionary.

Follow the guidelines in the previous chapters regarding soil preparation, fertilizing, and general garden care when tending flower beds. When growing annuals, incorporate fertilizer into the ground before planting. Unless it is so noted in the plant dictionary that a particular annual needs further fertilizing, this first feeding will be sufficient. Perennials should be fertilized when growth starts in early to mid-spring. Again, unless it is so noted in the plant dictionary, perennials will not need further feeding. It is possible that taller annuals and perennials will need to be staked.

When perennials become crowded or cease to bloom properly or if the center of the plant dies out, they should be dug up and divided. This can be done in either spring or autumn, except for those perennials that must be planted in autumn. Winter protection may need to be applied if a perennial is grown near the limits of its hardiness.

With flower growing, more than with any other type of gardening, neatness is a must. Remove flowers as soon as they fade to keep the garden in tip-top condition and to encourage further bloom. When frost has killed the tops of flowering plants, cut the tops off of perennials at ground level and remove annuals from their beds and borders. This is not only for appearance's sake; it also removes the overwintering havens for many insects and diseases.

*Formal gardens (BELOW) call for straight lines and geometric patterns.*

*When designing a flower bed or border (TOP RIGHT), vary the size and texture of the plants.*

*A border along the front of the house (BOTTOM RIGHT) will be enjoyed by both visitors and passersby.*

## ■ DESIGNING WITH ANNUALS AND PERENNIALS

Designing with annuals and perennials involves determining the size and shape of planting beds or borders, locating them to their best advantage, using them with other plants, and choosing plants for their size, shape, time of flowering, and flower and foliage color.

Flower beds are plantings that are accessible and viewed from all sides. An example is an island bed in the middle of the lawn. The size of a flower bed depends on the size and scale of the property and should take up no more than one third of the total area to look in proportion. Beds that are formal in design are usually square, rectangular, or some other symmetrical

shape with straight sides. Informal beds have curved sides and are rounded or free-form. Your choice will depend on the architecture of your house and the look you want to achieve.

Borders are plantings at the edge of an area and are accessible from three sides at the most. They back up onto the house, a wall, a fence, or a planting of shrubs or trees. To keep a border in scale and proportion to its surroundings, make it no wider than one third its length. However, since borders can be worked from only one side, they should be no wider than 5 feet (1.5m) or it will be difficult to care for them.

# THE NATURAL FLOWER GARDEN

*Plant wildflowers and grasses (LEFT) for a natural, easy-care border.*

The location of beds and borders depends on several factors. Select spots on your property where you can see and enjoy them, from both inside and outside the house. Plantings at the front of the house allow passersby and visitors to share in the enjoyment of your flowers. Look at such existing, permanent features as the house, trees, driveways, walkways, and boundary lines between you and your neighbors, and work the beds and borders into them so that they complement each other.

Your imagination is the only limiting factor. Plant flowers along garden paths; in front of fences and walls; along the patio, porch, or deck; in window boxes; next to garden benches; around the bases of trees; under shrubs; at the base of the mailbox or an outside light. They can be used to attract the eye to a focal point in the garden or to camouflage eyesores. If you're new to gardening, start small; you can always add to your plantings in following years if you find that you have the time to maintain a larger garden.

Think about using flowers for special effects. Flowering vines are without equal as screens on fences, walls, trellises, or arbors. They can be used for privacy or to block out unsightly views such as the work area, gas tanks, or refuse storage areas. In newly planted landscapes, low-growing annuals can be used as temporary quick covers while the permanent shrubs, ground covers, and perennials mature.

Patios are especially comfortable when lined with borders of flowers. To enhance them even more, set containers of annuals in the corners, next to the lounge chairs, or along the steps into the house. When the containers are planted with fragrant flowers, life on the patio will be even more enriched. Annuals in hanging baskets brighten the sky and create a colorful ceiling in the garden.

You can plant a special cutting garden or, if space does not allow, use flowers in beds and borders whose blooms make good cut flowers so you will have bouquets to brighten the inside of the house.

*Try vine-covered trellises (LEFT) to create an accent, hide an unsightly view, or direct garden traffic.*

*Variety (BELOW) is the
spice of life as well as of
the flower border.*

Annuals can be used in gardens to create geometric designs or to spell out your name. Before planting, lay out the design on the ground. Select annuals with contrasting foliage or flower color so the design will be visible, and use annuals whose growth habit is compact so the design will remain intact through the season. Good choices for annuals to usc in designs are begonias, marigolds, sweet alyssum, phlox, and salvia. Perennials do not work as well as annuals in designs because of their more limited period of bloom.

The next step in creating the garden is to decide which flowers to plant. First make a list of which ones it is possible to grow, based on fulfilling your climatic conditions of light, temperature, and water availability, and with perennials, hardiness (see the zone map on page 186). With perennials, you will also want to consider time of bloom so that there is always a selection of two that will be in flower throughout the season. The plant listings that appear later in this chapter outline the light, heat, and water requirements of the most common annuals, perennials, and biennials, and for perennials, the listings also denote hardiness and season of bloom.

Next decide which of these you want to grow. Narrowing down the list depends on plant height, plant shape, type of foliage, season of bloom, and flower colors you want to include, along with other considerations such as having flowers for cutting, drying, fragrance, or insect-repelling capabilities. If a plant is particularly prone to an insect or disease, you may want to disregard it if that insect or disease is a problem in your area. For example, mildew-prone flowers such as zinnias and phlox would not be a good choice for cool, damp gardens, which encourage the growth of this disease.

© Stephen Bitti

Whether you plant beds and borders with one type of plant or a mixture of plants depends on several factors. Small beds or narrow borders usually look best with low-growing plants of the same type. However, a small bed planted with only, say, irises, will have no appeal after early summer when the irises stop blooming. Ringing the bed with annuals will correct this. In larger plantings, a variety of heights is more interesting than having everything the same height. The

*Majestic foxgloves (RIGHT) are complemented by lower-growing primulas.*

© Charles Mann

tallest plants should be at the back of the border or the center of the bed, scaling down to low-growing plants at the front or the edges. Against a tall hedge or fence, plant tall flowers, working down to ground-hugging plants in the front.

Plants generally come in three shapes: spiked, rounded, or prostrate. A combination of all three shapes within a mixed border or bed is most attractive. This same combination of plant forms is also effective for plantings in containers and window boxes. Annuals are the best choice for planters because, almost without exception, they have a season-long period of bloom.

It is most effective to design beds and borders so that there are groupings of at least three plants of a kind, unless the plants are very large. Repetition of the same plants throughout the bed or border brings continuity and flow.

Color is a most critical aspect of flower-bed design. It reflects your personality and the personality of your home. Choose a color scheme to avoid a look that is too busy and distracting, which happens when you plant every color in the rainbow. A warm scheme, made up of red, orange, gold, and yellow tones is exciting, happy, and cheerful. It draws the eye to the garden and makes it look smaller than it really is. It also makes a garden appear to be hotter than it is. A cool scheme, which is comprised of green, blue, violet, and purple, is cooling, soothing, and calming. It makes a small garden look larger and is good when used to hide an eyesore because it does not draw attention. It is also the best choice for a quiet garden for reading or relaxing.

Buy a color wheel at an art supply store to help you select color harmonies. Those colors that are across the wheel from each other, such as purple and yellow, are complementary colors. This is a strong harmony and may be too overpowering for a small garden. In split complementary harmony, the first color is used with a color that is on either side of its opposite. In this case, you would use yellow with either blue or red. Analagous harmony uses three colors in a row on the wheel, such as yellow, gold, and orange or tones of blues and violets. Since perennials have short blooming periods, it is possible to have three different color schemes during one growing season—one for spring, one for summer, and a third for autumn.

It is best to start with one color as the primary color and use one or at most two different colors with it. Once you gain experience, you will know if you can safely add more colors without creating a distracting look.

Monochromatic harmony is another type of color scheme that uses only different shades and tones of the same color. To avoid monotony, use different types of plants, such as yellow marigolds, yellow zinnias, and yellow coreopsis. You could also choose one type of plant, such as impatiens or phlox, and choose varieties with differing shades.

*Keep cool and calm with flowers (ABOVE) in the blue to purple color range.*

*Combine golden* Achillea *'Moonshine' and purple* Geranium *(ABOVE RIGHT) to create complementary color harmony.*

© Grace Davies/Envision

*Think beyond flowers (OPPOSITE) and look for unusually shaped or colored foliage when designing a flower garden.*

*Early spring-blooming perennials (LEFT) form a delicate carpet for stately tulips.*

Pink is a tone of red, so it is used in the same way as red. It is an excellent color for a garden that will be viewed at night, as is white, for dark colors will fade into the background after sunset. Pastels in the night garden also add visibility to garden paths.

White can be used on its own or as a buffer or unifying color in the garden. If you use only one plant here and another one there, it will give a spotty look, so use white in mass or as a unifying border. Plants with white, silver, or gray leaves are used in the same way as plants with white flowers.

Before making a final color selection, consider the color of the house, fence, or wall that the bed or border will be seen against, and make sure the colors are complementary.

Think beyond flower color and plant shape when deciding on your list of plants. Look also for a variety of foliage textures and colors. A mixture of large, coarse foliage with others that have finely cut leaves is most effective. Most plants have green leaves, but some have leaves of red, bronze, purple, silver, or gray that are useful for an accent. Treat these plants in the same way as plants with the same flower colors when you are designing your beds.

Annuals and perennials do not need to stand alone or be used only with each other, although they can be. Early-blooming plants can be combined with spring bulbs, while summer-flowering types can be effectively mixed with tender bulbs. Use annuals and perennials interplanted with roses or bordering a rose bed or with shrubs. Annuals can also be combined in the herb or vegetable garden to add more color and interest.

Think of how much maintenance you can give to the garden. When time is limited, pick plants that do not require pinching, are not subject to insect or disease problems, or have flowers that fall cleanly as they die, eliminating having to cut faded flowers off. Those annuals and perennials requiring the least amount of maintenance are designated in the plant list as *easy*.

When choosing annual varieties, you will note that some are sold in what is known as a series. For example, there are Super Elfin impatiens, Madness petunias, Boy marigolds, and Sprinter geraniums. Series contain plants of the same growth habit and size but with numerous different colors. Because of this characteristic, it is best when planting different colors of the same annual to choose plants from the same series so as to preserve uniformity of appearance.

# 🌿 A Dictionary of Annuals 🌿

Below are outlined the descriptions and growing requirements for the most popular annuals. They are listed in alphabetical order by the Latin name, followed by the common name. Next are the light, temperature, and soil moisture requirements, and the hardiness rating. Lastly, there is a description of the plant and any special care needs.

If a plant is listed as needing sun, it needs at least 6 hours of sun a day. Partial shade is 4 to 6 hours of sun a day, and shade is less than 4 hours of sun. Cool temperatures are below 70°F (21°C), average temperatures are 70°F to 85°F (21°C to 30°C), and hot temperatures are over 85°F (30°C). If a plant needs dry soil, allow the top inch of soil to become dry before watering. If a plant has average water requirements, water when the soil surface becomes dry. When moist soil is needed, never let the soil surface dry out. An annual's rating falls into one of three categories: tender (plants should not be planted until all danger of frost is gone and the ground is warm, and they will die with the first frost of autumn); half-hardy (plants will not survive frost but can be planted during the cool weather of early spring); and hardy (plants will withstand some frost and can be planted in late autumn or early spring).

*Ageratum*

## *Ageratum houstonianum*
Ageratum, floss flower

■ *Sun to partial shade; average temperatures; average to moist soil; half-hardy*

■ Predominantly blue, but sometimes pink or white fluffy flowers smother mounded 4- to 8-inch (10- to 20cm) plants. Set purchased or indoor-started plants 5 to 7 inches (12.5 to 17.5cm) apart. Fertilize monthly. Easy.

© Anita Sabarese

*Flowering cabbage*

## *Antirrhinum majus*
Snapdragon

■ *Sun; cool to average temperatures; average soil moisture; hardy*

■ Intriguing, fragrant flowers in mixed colors bloom in spikes on 6- to 30-inch (15 to 75cm) plants. Sow seeds outdoors or set plants 6 to 8 inches (15 to 20cm) apart; do not overcrowd to discourage disease. Fertilize monthly.

## *Begonia sempervirens-cultorum*
Wax begonia

■ *Partial shade to shade; average temperatures; average soil moisture; half-hardy*

■ Mounds of white, pink, or red flowers cover 6- to 8-inch (15 to 20cm) plants with waxy leaves. Set purchased or indoor-started plants 7 to 9 inches (17.5 to 22.5cm) apart; start seeds indoors 12 to 16 weeks before planting outside. Begonias can also be grown from stem cuttings. Fertilize monthly. Easy.

## *Brassica oleracea*
Flowering cabbage or kale

■ *Sun; cool temperatures; moist soil; hardy*

■ Set purchased or indoor-started plants 15 to 18 inches (37.5 to 45cm) apart in early autumn for autumn and winter displays of white, purple, or pink rosettes of foliage on 15- to 18-inch (37.5 to 45cm) plants. Fertilize monthly. Easy.

## Calendula officinalis
Pot marigold

- *Sun to partial shade; cool to average temperatures; moist soil; hardy*
- Yellow or orange daisies brighten 10- to 20-inch (25 to 50cm) plants. Sow seeds outdoors or set plants 8 to 10 (20 to 25cm) apart. Calendula flowers are edible. Repels nematodes.

## Callistephus chinensis
China aster

- *Sun to partial shade; average temperatures; half-hardy*
- Flowers of mixed colors top 6- to 30-inch (15 to 75cm) plants. Sow seeds outdoors or set plants 6 to 18 inches (15 to 45cm) apart. Rotate planting sites to discourage disease. Fertilize monthly.

## Capsicum annuum
Ornamental pepper

- *Sun to partial shade; average to hot temperatures; moist soil; half-hardy*
- Tiny white flowers are followed by red, yellow, orange, or purple fruits on 4- to 8-inch (10 to 20cm) plants. Set purchased or indoor-grown plants 5 to 7 inches (12.5 to 17.5cm) apart. Do not overfertilize —it discourages fruit formation. Easy.

## Catharanthus roseus
Vinca, periwinkle

- *Sun to partial shade; average to hot temperatures; dry to moist soil; half-hardy*
- Flat flowers of white, rose, or pink cover erect or trailing plants 4 to 12 inches (10 to 30cm) high.

*Pot marigolds*

Set purchased or indoor-grown plants 6 to 8 inches (15 to 20cm) apart, starting seeds indoors 12 weeks before planting. Vinca can also be grown from stem cuttings. Easy.

## *Celosia cristata*
### Cockscomb
■ *Sun; average to hot temperatures; dry soil; tender*
■ Flowers in mixed, almost bizarre colors are either plumed or rounded. Plant height varies from 6 to 20 inches (15 to 50cm). Start seeds outdoors or set plants 6 to 10 inches (15 to 25cm) apart.

## *Cleome basslerana*
### Spider flower
■ *Sun; average to hot temperatures; dry soil; half-hardy*
■ Pink or white spidery, scented flowers top back-of-the-border 30- to 48-inch (75 to 120cm) plants. Start seeds outdoors or set plants 12 to 15 inches (30 to 37.5cm) apart. Feed very lightly. Easy.

## *Coleus* × *hybridus*
### Coleus
■ *Partial shade to shade; average to hot temperatures; average to moist soil; tender*
■ Although spikes of blue flowers form in late summer, coleus is grown for its brightly colored foliage. Plants grow 10 to 24 inches (25 to 60cm) high. Set purchased or indoor-grown plants 8 to 10 inches (20 to 25cm) apart. Coleus can also be grown from stem cuttings. Fertilize every other month. Easy.

## *Cosmos bipinnatus, Cosmos sulphureus*
### Cosmos
■ *Sun; average temperatures; dry to average soil; half-hardy*
■ *C. bipinnatus* has lavender, pink, red, or white flowers on 30- to 48-inch (75 to 120cm) plants with lacy foliage; *C. sulphureus* has orange or yellow flowers on 12- to 36-inch (30 to 90cm) plants. Sow seeds outdoors or set plants 9 to 18 inches (22.5 to 45cm) apart. Fertilize lightly.

*Cosmos*

*Sunflower*

© Charles Mann

### Gazania rigens
Treasure flower

■ *Sun; average to hot temperatures; dry to average soil; half-hardy*

■ Gold, yellow, or orange daisies top ground-hugging, 6-inch (15cm) plants. Sow seeds outdoors or set plants 8 to 10 inches (20 to 37.5cm) apart.

### Helianthus annuus
Sunflower

■ *Sun; hot temperatures; dry soil; tender*

■ Yellow flowers top plants that can grow from 15 inches (37.5cm) to 12 feet (3.6m) tall. Sow seeds outdoors or set plants 12 to 24 inches (30 to 60cm) apart. Fertilize lightly.

### Iberis species
Candytuft

■ *Sun; cool to hot temperatures; dry to average soil; half-hardy*

■ White, pink, or lavender flowers (some with fragrance) smother upright or mounded plants growing 6 to 10 inches (15 to 25cm) high. Sow seeds outdoors or set plants 7 to 9 inches (17.5 to 22.5cm) apart. Easy.

### Dianthus chinensis
China pink

■ *Sun to partial shade; cool to average temperatures; average soil; half-hardy*

■ Pink, red, or white fragrant flowers cover 6- to 18-inch (15 to 45cm) plants. Set purchased or indoor-grown plants 7 to 10 inches (17.5 to 25cm) apart. Prefers alkaline soil. Fertilize monthly. Easy.

### Gaillardia pulchella
Blanketflower

■ *Sun; average to hot temperatures; dry to average soil; half-hardy*

■ Red or orange two-toned flowers bloom on 10- to 18-inch (25 to 45cm) plants. Sow seeds outdoors or set plants 8 to 15 inches (20 to 37.5cm) apart. Fertilize very lightly.

*Morning glories*

## Lathyrus odoratus
Sweet pea
- *Sun; cool to average temperatures; moist soil; hardy*
- Vines growing to 5 feet (1.5m) or more, or 2-foot (60cm) bushy plants have flowers in mixed colors. Sow seeds outdoors and thin plants 6 to 15 inches (15 to 37.5 cm) apart. Fixes nitrogen in the soil.

## Impatiens wallerana
Impatiens
- *Partial shade to shade; average temperatures; moist soil; tender*
- Flowers in almost any color cover 6- to 18-inch (15 to 45.5cm) plants. Set purchased or indoor-started plants 8 to 10 inches (20 to 25cm) apart, starting seeds indoors 10 to 14 weeks before planting. Impatiens can also be grown from stem cuttings. Fertilize lightly. Easy.

## Ipomoea species
Morning glory
- *Sun; average temperatures; moist soil; tender*
- Either a 3-foot (0.9m) bush or a vine that can grow 30 feet (9m), morning glories come in a variety of colors. Sow seeds outdoors or set plants 12 to 18 inches (30 to 45cm) apart.

## Lobelia erinus
Lobelia
- *Sun to partial shade; cool to average temperatures; moist soil, half-hardy*
- Bright blue or purple flowers hug 3- to 5-inch (7.5 to 12.5cm) plants. Set purchased or indoor-grown plants 8 to 10 inches (20 to 25cm) apart, starting seeds indoors 10 to 12 weeks before planting. Easy.

## Lobularia maritima
Sweet alyssum
- *Sun to partial shade; average temperatures; average to moist soil; hardy*
- White, pink, or lavender flowers with a delicious fragrance cover 3- to 6-inch (7.5 to 15cm) plants. Sow seeds outdoors or set plants 10 to 12 inches (25 to 30cm) apart. Easy.

### Nicotiana alata
Flowering tobacco

■ *Sun to partial shade; average to hot temperatures; average to moist soil; half-hardy*

■ Mixed colors appear in spikes on 12- to 15-inch (30 to 37.5cm) plants. Sow seeds outdoors or set plants 8 to 10 inches (20 to 25cm) apart. Easy.

### Pelargonium × hortorum
Geranium

■ *Sun; average temperatures; average to moist soil; tender*

■ Globular flowers of various colors appear above 10- to 15-inch (25 to 37.5cm) plants. Set purchased or indoor-grown plants 10 to 12 inches (25 to 30cm) apart, starting seeds indoors 12 to 16 weeks before planting. Geraniums can also be grown from stem cuttings. Fertilize monthly. Repels leafhoppers.

### Petunia × hybrida
Petunia

■ *Sun; average to hot temperatures; dry soil; half-hardy*

■ Single or double flowers in all colors bloom on 6- to 12-inch (15 to 25cm) plants. Set purchased or indoor-grown plants 10 to 12 (25 to 30cm) apart, starting seeds 10 to 12 weeks before planting. Grandiflora types are prone to botrytis; multiflora types are not. Repels leafhoppers and Mexican bean beetles.

*Gloriosa daisy*

## *Phlox drummondi*
### Annual phlox

- *Sun; cool to average temperatures; moist soil; hardy*
- Multiple colors bloom on 6- to 10-inch (15 to 25cm) plants. Sow seeds outdoors or set purchased or indoor-grown plants 7 to 9 inches (17.5 to 22.5cm) apart, starting seeds indoors 10 weeks before planting time. Fertilize monthly. Easy.

## *Portulaca grandiflora*
### Moss rose

- *Sun; hot temperatures; dry soil; tender*
- Single or double flowers in a rainbow of colors bloom on sunny days on trailing 4- to 6-inch (10 to 15cm) plants. Sow seeds outdoors or set plants 6 to 8 inches (15 to 25cm) apart, starting seeds indoors 10 weeks before planting time. Easy.

## *Rudbeckia hirta*
### Gloriosa daisy

- *Sun; average to hot temperatures; average soil; half-hardy*
- Gold or yellow daisies bloom on 18- to 36-inch (45 to 90cm) plants. Sow seeds outdoors or set plants 12 to 24 inches (30 to 60cm) apart. Easy.

*Flowering tobacco (LEFT)*

## *Salvia splendens*
### Scarlet sage

- *Sun to partial shade; average to hot temperatures; average to moist soil; half-hardy*
- Spikes of red, purple, or white bloom on 12- to 24-inch (30 to 60cm) plants. Set purchased or indoor-grown plants 6 to 8 inches (15 to 25cm) apart, starting seeds indoors 8 to 10 weeks earlier. Feed lightly every month. Repels nematodes. Easy.

## *Sanvitalia procumbens*
### Creeping zinnia

- *Sun; average to hot temperatures; dry to average soil; half-hardy*
- Yellow or orange daisies cover trailing 4- to 8-inch (10 to 20cm) plants. Sow seeds outdoors or set plants 5 to 7 inches (12.5 to 17.5cm) apart.

## *Tagetes erecta*
### African marigold

- *Sun; average temperatures; average soil; half-hardy*
- Globular flowers of gold, yellow, or orange top 18- to 30-inch (45 to 75cm) plants. Set purchased or indoor-grown plants 12 to 15 inches (30 to 37.5cm) apart. Most will not bloom until late summer unless planted in bud or bloom. Fertilize monthly. Repels a large number of insects.

*Pansies*

## *Tagetes patula*
French marigold

- *Sun; average temperatures; average soil; half-hardy*
- Gold, yellow, orange, or red flowers bloom on 5- to 10-inch (12.5 to 25cm) plants. Sow seeds outdoors or set plants 3 to 6 inches (7.5 to 15cm) apart. Fertilize monthly. Repels a large number of insects and nematodes.

## *Tropaeolum majus*
Nasturtium

- *Sun; cool to average temperatures; dry soil; tender*
- Yellow, orange, or red flowers bloom on mounded or trailing plants 12 to 24 inches (30 to 60cm) high. Sow seeds outdoors and thin to 8 to 12 inches (20 to 30cm) apart. Fertilize lightly. Repels many insects but attracts aphids. Easy.

## *Viola* × *wittrockiana*
Pansy

- *Sun to partial shade; cool temperatures; moist soil; hardy*
- Flowers in a rainbow of colors appear on 4- to 8-inch (10 to 20cm) plants. Set purchased or indoor-grown plants 6 to 8 inches (15 to 20cm) apart, starting seeds indoors 14 weeks before planting time. Fertilize monthly.

## *Zinnia elegans*
Zinnia

- *Sun; average to hot temperatures; dry to average soil; tender*
- Single or double daisies in many colors bloom on 4- to 36-inch (10 to 90cm) plants. Sow seeds outdoors or set plants 4 to 24 inches (10 to 60cm) apart. Prone to mildew.

*Nasturtium*

# A Dictionary of Perennials and Biennials

Below are outlined the descriptions and growing requirements for the most popular perennials. They are listed in alphabetical order by the Latin name, followed by the common name. Next are the light, temperature, and soil moisture requirements, and the hardiness rating. Lastly, there is a description of the plant and any special care needs.

If a plant is listed as needing sun, it needs at least 6 hours of sun a day. Partial shade is 4 to 6 hours of sun a day, and shade is less than 4 hours of sun. Cool temperatures are below 70°F (21°C), average temperatures are 70°F to 85°F (21°C to 30°C), and hot temperatures are over 85°F (30°C). If a plant needs dry soil, allow the top inch of soil to become dry before watering. If a plant has average water requirements, water when the soil surface becomes dry. When moist soil is needed, never let the soil surface dry out. Compare the zones listed for each perennial with the hardiness zone map on page 186.

## *Achillea* species
### Yarrow
- *Sun; average to hot temperatures; dry soil; zones 3–9*
- Flat heads of yellow, white, or magenta flowers top 2- to 3-foot (60 to 90cm) plants in early

summer and sometimes again in early autumn. Set plants, which have fernlike foliage, 1 to 2 feet (30 to 60cm) apart. Easy.

## *Alcea rosea*
### Hollyhock
- *Sun; average temperatures; moist soil; zones 3–8*
- Almost looking like paper flowers, large blooms in a variety of colors appear in early summer on 4- to 10-foot (1.2 to 3m) spikes. Space plants, which have coarse foliage, 1½ feet (45cm) apart. Hollyhocks are prone to rust. Biennial but act as perennial because they quickly self-sow from dropped seeds.

© Charles Mann

*Hollybocks*

## *Aster* species
### Aster

- *Sun; average temperatures; average soil; zones 2–8*
- A traditional flower of late summer and autumn, asters have daisylike flowers in many colors on 2- to 8-foot (60cm to 2.4m) plants. Set plants 1 to 3 feet (30 to 90cm) apart.

## *Astilbe* species
### Astilbe

- *Sun to partial shade; average temperatures; average to moist soil; zones 4–8*
- Plumes of pink, white, or red appear in early summer on 1- to 3- foot (30 to 90cm) plants that have ferny foliage. Allow a planting distance of 1 to 2 feet (30 to 60cm). Easy.

## *Aquilegia* species
### Columbine

- *Sun to partial shade; cool to average temperatures; average to moist soil; zones 3–9*
- Unusual flowers with long spurs bloom in a variety of colors, sometimes two-toned, in late spring. Plants are 1 to 3 feet (30 to 90cm) high and should be spaced 1¹/₂ feet (45cm) apart. Easy.

*Astilbe*

## *Baptisia australis*
### Blue false indigo

- *Sun; cool to average temperatures; average to dry soil; zones 3–8*
- Shrubby 3- to 4-foot (90 to 120cm) plants are covered with blue flowers in late spring. Set plants 2 to 3 feet (60 to 90cm) apart. Fixes nitrogen in the soil.

*Coreopsis*

© Stephen Bitti

## Bellis perennis
English daisy

■ *Sun to partial shade; cool temperatures; moist soil; zones 3–7*

■ Tiny white, pink, or red daisies bloom 6 inches (15cm) over tufted foilage in late spring and early summer. Plant 6 inches (15cm) apart. Biennial.

## Campanula species
Bellflower

■ *Sun to partial shade; average temperatures; average to moist soil; zones 3–9*

■ Blue or white bell- or star-shaped flowers appear from late spring to midsummer on plants ranging from 6 inches (15cm) to 5 feet (1.5m) in height. Space 6 inches (15cm) to 2 feet (60cm) apart, depending on plant size.

## Chelone lyonii
Turtlehead

■ *Sun to partial shade; average temperatures; moist soil; zones 4–9*

■ Spikes of pink flowers that resemble a turtle's head bloom in late summer and fall on 3- to 4-foot (90 to 120cm) plants that should be set 2 feet (60cm) apart. Easy.

## Chrysanthemum species

■ *Sun; average temperatures; average to moist soil; zones 3–10*

■ Flowers in a multitude of shapes, sizes, and colors bloom in late summer and autumn. Many newer varieties need no artificial shading to bloom by late summer. Depending on plant size, which can vary from 6 inches (15cm) to 5 feet (1.5m), space plants 6 inches (15cm) to 2 feet (60cm) apart. Fertilize in early to mid-spring and again in early summer and midsummer.

Delphinium

*Charles Mann*

### *Coreopsis* species
### Coreopsis

■ *Sun; average to hot temperatures; average to moist soil; zones 3–10*

■ Yellow daisies bloom from early to late summer on 1½- to 3-foot (45 to 90cm) plants, making this one of the longest-blooming perennials. Plants should be set 1 to 1½ feet apart (30 to 45cm). Easy.

### *Delphinium* species
### Delphinium

■ *Sun; average temperatures; moist soil; zones 3–8*

■ Flowers in tones of white through blue and purple bloom in early summer on 1- to 6-foot (30cm to 1.8m) spikes. Space plants 2 feet (60cm) apart in a slightly alkaline soil.

© Charles Mann

*Bleeding hearts (LEFT)*        *Foxglove (RIGHT)*

## *Digitalis purpurea*
### Foxglove

- *Sun to partial shade; average temperatures; average to moist soil; zones 4–7*
- Flowers in a variety of colors resemble the fingertips of a glove and bloom in late spring and early summer. Plants grow 3 to 7 feet (90cm to 2.1m) high and should be planted 15 to 24 inches (37.5 to 60cm) apart. Biennial.

## *Dracocephalum virginianum*
### False dragonhead

- *Sun; average temperatures; moist soil; zones 4–9*
- Formerly called *Physostegia virginiana*, this perennial has 2- to 5-foot (60cm to 1.5m) spikes of pink flowers in late summer. Allow a planting distance of 1¹/₂ to 2 feet (45 to 60cm). Easy.

## *Echinacea purpurea*
### Purple coneflower

- *Sun to partial shade; average temperatures; average to dry soil; zones 3–10*
- Purple daisies with drooping petals bloom in midsummer on 2- to 4-foot (60cm to 1.2m) plants. Set plants 2 feet (60cm) apart. Easy.

## *Dicentra* species
### Bleeding heart

- *Partial shade; average temperatures; moist soil; zones 3–9*
- Heart-shaped pink flowers hang gracefully from arching branches on 2- to 3-foot (60 to 90cm) plants. *D. spectabilis* blooms in midspring and has large leaves that fall by midsummer; *D. exima* has smaller flowers that bloom from midspring into summer and finer foliage that does not fall from the plant. Space 1¹/₂ to 2 feet (30 to 60cm) apart. Easy.

© Charles Mann

*Globe thistle*

© Charles Mann

© Charles Mann

## *Echinops ritro*
### Globe thistle

■ *Sun; average to hot temperatures; dry soil; zones 3–9*

■ Globe-shaped purple flowers bloom in midsummer on prickly 2- to 4-foot (60cm to 1.2m) plants. Space 1¹/₂ to 2 feet (45 to 60cm) apart. Easy.

## *Gaillardia* × *grandiflora*
### Blanket flower

■ *Sun; average to hot temperatures; dry soil; zones 3–11*

■ Two-toned daisies of red and yellow bloom from early to late summer on 1- to 3-foot (30 to 90cm) plants, making this one of the few perennials with a long blooming season. Plant 1¹/₂ feet (45cm) apart. It is excellent for a seashore garden. Easy.

## *Geranium* species
### Cranesbill

■ *Sun to partial shade; average temperatures; moist soil; zones 3–10*

■ The true geranium (although the annual geranium is related), this perennial has flowers primarily of pink or blue on 6-inch to 1-foot (15 to 30cm) plants that bloom in late spring. Space 1 foot (30cm) apart. Easy.

## *Helleborus* species
### Christmas or Lenten rose

■ *Partial shade to shade; cool temperatures; moist soil; zones 3–8*

■ The Christmas rose, *Helleborus niger*, blooms in autumn or winter and has white flowers; Lenten rose, *H. orientalis*, blooms in late winter and has cream, rose, or purple flowers. Plants grow 12 to 18 inches (30 to 45cm) high and should be spaced 1¹/₂ to 2 feet (45 to 60cm) apart.

## *Hemerocallis* species
### Daylily

■ *Partial shade; average temperatures; average soil; zones 3–9*

■ Lily-shaped flowers in many colors but primarily yellow, orange, and red last for only one day, but the blooming period of different varieties spans from early to late summer. Plants vary from 1 to 6 feet (15cm to 1.8m) in height, have grassy foliage, and should be spaced 1 to 3 feet (30 to 90cm) apart. Easy.

*Cranesbill geranium*

## *Hosta* species
### Plantain lily, funkia

■ *Partial shade; average temperatures; moist soil; zones 3–9*

■ Grown mostly for its ground-hugging foliage, which varies in size, texture, and color, plantain lily has 6-inch to 3-foot (15 to 90cm) spikes of white to lavender flowers in mid- to late summer. Plant this ground cover 1 to 2 feet (30 to 60cm) apart. Easy.

## *Iris × germanica*
### Bearded iris

■ *Sun; average temperatures; average to dry soil; zones 3–9*

■ Stately flowers with three upright petals called standards and three drooping petals called falls bloom in a variety of colors in early summer. Plants range from 1 to 4 feet (30cm to 1.2m) tall and should be planted in autumn 1 foot (30cm) apart. There are also related species, the Japanese, Siberian, and crested irises. Fertilize in spring and again after blooming has finished. Bearded iris prefers slightly alkaline soil.

*Lupine*

### *Liatris spicata*
Blazing star

■ *Sun; average temperatures; moist soil; zones 3–9*
■ Fuzzy spikes of purple flowers bloom on bushy
3- to 6-foot (90cm to 1.8m) plants in late summer.
Space 1 to 2 feet apart (30 to 60cm). Easy.

### *Lupinus* species
Lupine

■ *Sun; cool to average temperatures; moist soil; zones 3–9*
■ Thick spikes of flowers in mixed colors appear
on bushy 3- to 4-foot (90cm to 1.2m) plants in
late spring. Foliage is deeply cut. Plant 2 feet
(60cm) apart.

Better Homes & Gardens

### Lythrum salicaria
Purple loosestrife

■ *Sun; average temperatures; moist soil; zones 3–9*

■ Wispy spikes of pink to purple flowers bloom in midsummer on 3- to 4-foot (90cm to 1.2m) plants spaced 1¹/₂ to 2 feet (45 to 60cm) apart. Easy. Can be invasive; illegal in some states.

### Paeonia officinalis
Peony

■ *Sun; average temperatures; average soil; zones 3–8*

■ Single to fully double flowers in a mixture of colors bloom in early summer on 2- to 4-foot (60cm to 1.2m) plants. Plant roots 3 feet (90cm) apart and 1 inch (2.5cm) deep, and plant only in autumn. Fertilize again in spring and when flower buds are visible.

*Peonies*

### Papaver orientalis
Oriental poppy

■ *Sun; average to cool temperatures; dry soil; zones 3–9*

■ Brightly colored flowers with black centers bloom in early summer on 3- to 4-foot (90cm to 1.2m) plants. Foliage dies down during the summer and reappears in autumn. Plant or move in autumn, spacing 8 to 12 inches (20 to 30cm) apart.

### Phlox paniculata
Phlox

■ *Sun; average temperatures; dry soil; zones 3–9*

■ Large heads of tiny flowers bloom in midsummer in a variety of colors on 3- to 4-foot plants. Plant 2 feet (60cm) apart; do not overcrowd, as phlox is susceptible to mildew. Easy.

Violas *(RIGHT)*

### *Primula* species

■ *Partial shade; cool temperatures; moist soil; zones 3–10*

■ Flowers in a variety of colors bloom in clusters in early spring on 6-inch (15cm) to 3-foot (90cm) plants. Set 6 inches (15cm) to 1 foot (30cm) apart.

### *Rudbeckia fulgida*
Black-eyed Susan

■ *Sun; average to hot temperatures; dry soil; zones 3–9*

■ Bright yellow daisies with black centers bloom on 2- to 3-foot (60 to 90cm) plants during midsummer. Space 1 to 1¹/₂ feet (30 to 45cm) apart. Easy.

### *Sedum* species
Stonecrop

■ *Sun; average to hot temperatures; average to dry soil; zones 3–10*

■ Succulent plants with varicolored flowers range in height from 3 inches (7.5cm) to 2 feet (60cm). Some bloom in mid-spring, others in late summer. Space 1 to 2 feet (30 to 60cm) apart. Easy.

### *Solidago* species
Goldenrod

■ *Sun; average to hot temperatures; average to dry soil; zones 3–9*

■ Improvements to this wildflower have given us 2- to 5-foot (60cm to 1.5m) plants topped with plumy clusters of yellow flowers in late summer and autumn. Plant 1¹/₂ to 2 feet (45 to 60cm) apart. Easy.

### *Trillium* species
Wake robin

■ *Partial shade; average to cool temperatures; moist soil; zones 3–8*

■ Some flowers in this species are white, others are purple. Plants bloom in mid-spring and grow ¹/₂ to 1¹/₂ feet (15 to 45cm) tall. Plant 1 foot (30cm) apart.

### *Trollius europaeus*
Globeflower

■ *Partial shade; average to cool temperatures; moist soil; zones 3–10*

■ Golden globes bloom in mid-spring on 1¹/₂-foot (45cm) plants. Spacing should be 1 foot (30cm).

*Black-eyed Susans*

© Charles Mann

### *Veronica spicata*
Speedwell

- *Sun; average temperatures; moist soil; zones 3–8*
- Spikes of blue to purple flowers bloom on 1- to 3-foot (30 to 90cm) plants in early summer. Set 1 foot (30cm) apart.

### *Viola* species
Violet

- *Partial shade; cool to average temperatures; moist soil; zones 3–9*
- Perky "faces" bloom in mixed colors in mid-spring on 6-inch (15cm) to 1-foot (30cm) plants. Plant 6 inches (15cm) apart. Easy.

*Chapter Six*

# THE NATURAL
# VEGETABLE GARDEN

© Jerry Pavia

*Sunshine bathes a vegeta-ble garden designed for a diversity of crops.*

Although vegetable gardening is one of the most demanding types of gardening, it can also be one of the most rewarding. There is no denying that slicing into a fresh melon, sinking your teeth into a cherry tomato picked fresh from the vine, or creating a ratatouille from the fresh vegetables in your summer garden far outweighs the extra care a vegetable garden might demand over a flower or herb garden. A tremendous sense of satisfaction comes from serving nutritious fresh vegetables that you've grown yourself. There's also the added relief that you don't have to worry about the presence of harmful chemicals. If your vegetable garden yields more than the family can use in the summer, the surplus can be canned, frozen, or dried for enjoyment into the winter.

Most vegetables are annual plants—growing, flowering, developing the edible crop, and dying within one growing season. In the dictionary section that follows, all of the entries are annuals unless otherwise specified. Some vegetables are technically biennials but are grown as annuals because their taste and/or texture is better when they are young. Only a handful of vegetables are truly perennial.

Like flowering annuals, vegetables are classified as tender, half-hardy, or hardy. Tender vegetables will not tolerate frost and cannot be planted until all danger of frost has passed and the weather is stable and warm. Half-hardy vegetables will not tolerate frost but will grow during cool weather of spring and/or autumn. Hardy vegetables will tolerate frost and can be planted in early spring or for harvesting in autumn.

You will note that each of the entries in the following dictionary is designated either a cool-season or a warm-season vegetable. A cool-season vegetable is either a hardy or half-hardy vegetable best grown during the cool days of spring or autumn when the temperatures are between 65°F (18°C) and 80°F (27°C). A warm-season vegetable flourishes only during the warm or hot days of summer when the temperature is above 75°F (24°C). As you can see, there is some overlap between the two.

## ■ DESIGNING THE VEGETABLE GARDEN

Whether you garden in the cool far reaches of Alaska or along the hot, humid borders of the Gulf of Mexico, several guidelines—along with some common sense—are necessary for selecting the proper site for your vegetable garden.

The first requirement for a vegetable garden is sunlight, and most vegetables like full sun or at least 6 hours of sunlight daily. Garden sites that lack full sun, however, can still produce some good vegetables. Leafy vegetables like lettuce and spinach grow well in 4 to 6 hours of sun a day. If you are growing an early-spring garden or a warm-season garden in a cool area, select the site with the most sun. These gardens will also benefit from reflected heat, such as that from a white wall or fence. If the climate is very hot, most vegetables will benefit from afternoon shade. Witness the prize-winning cabbages grown in Anchorage, Alaska, and you'll understand the impact long northern days have on vegetable size and speed of production.

After considering sunlight, a vegetable garden should be located where the air circulation is good (to discourage diseases), where the soil drains well, and away from large trees and shrubs (which may compete with the vegetables for food and water as well as cast too much shade). However, keep the vegetable garden out of direct wind. Many vegetables, such as peppers

*Create a living patchwork
quilt or checkerboard
(BELOW) with different
varieties of lettuce.*

and tomatoes, will not produce in very windy spots. If there is no other choice, block the wind with a living windbreak or a fence.

It is a wise idea to plan your garden on paper first. This allows you to plan for growing the largest number of vegetables in the available space and to plan for a succession of crops. If you're just beginning, start with a garden that measures approximately 15 by 20 feet (4.5 by 6m). After you have planned it out on paper, you'll know how many plants to grow or buy.

You can lay the garden out in either rows or in blocks. The latter method is sometimes called intensive gardening and is popular because it makes the most efficient use of garden space. Guidelines for spacing between plants are given in the dictionary and are the same whether you garden in rows or in blocks.

If you decide to grow vegetables in rows, the row should not be planted any wider than you can work it without having to step into the row and compact the soil. Depending on what is being grown, a row could be one plant wide, as with winter squash, or many plants wide, as with beets or carrots. Between rows, leave as much space as you need to walk and carry your garden equipment. Orient your rows in an east-west direction, and place the taller plants on the west side of the row so they will not shade the lower-growing ones until the afternoon.

If you plant in blocks, plan the garden so that you can reach into the center of the block without having to step on the soil. Between the blocks, leave enough space for walking and carrying equipment through. Raised beds are usually used in this type of planting so drainage will be excellent; raised beds also warm up earlier in spring than the ground does, extending the planting season somewhat.

Begin planning the garden by making a list of your —and your family's—favorite vegetables. Next, label each as cool season or warm season, and if cool season, whether it is grown in spring, autumn, or both. Next, working with the number of days to maturity specified in the dictionary (and also on the seed packets and/or plant labels), figure out how to include as many vegetables as possible to make the most use of your garden space. When planning an autumn crop, determine the number of days to maturity for that crop, and count backward from the total number of days in the growing season to determine the planting date for that crop. Some vegetables have such a long growing season that they will occupy their spot for the entire time. Your cooperative extension office can give you the dates of the first and last frosts and the number of days in the growing season for your particular area.

© Derek Fell

*Vegetables and raised beds
(BELOW) go hand in hand.*

© Derek Fell

*The timing for the direct sowing of radish seeds (LEFT) is staggered for a constant crop.*

Reread the section in chapter four about crop rotation, and note which vegetables should not be planted in the same spot in succeeding years to deter attacks by insects and diseases. Divide your garden into three or four sections, and rotate crops through these sections each year. Besides rotation based on insect and disease resistance, vegetables should also be rotated according to their fertilizer needs. It is best to first plant heavy feeders such as corn, cucumbers, pumpkins, or tomatoes (or any other vegetable that needs additional fertilizing after planting). Then, for the following planting, turn the space over to light feeders such as carrots, peppers, or Swiss chard (or any vegetable that needs little or no additional feeding after planting). In

You can plant peas, for example, in one section of the garden in early spring. By the time the peas are harvested, the space can be filled with tomatoes or brussels sprouts. In late summer, lettuce plants can be set between the tomatoes. Work out a similar plan with the remainder of the vegetables you want to grow.

Practice succession planting with vegetables that are harvested once, such as carrots and beets. Sowing seeds every two weeks instead of all at once will ensure a continuous supply of these vegetables throughout the growing season.

Interplanting is another way to make the most use of space. To do this, plant two crops together that will not interfere with each other's growth or space. For example, plant carrots or lettuce under or in between tomatoes. Any small vegetables, like beets and radishes, can be planted among almost any tall-growing plants; the shade the taller plant provides is often beneficial in keeping the other plants and the ground cool. Also mix shallow-rooted plants (cabbage and its relatives, celery, corn, endive, lettuce, onion and its relatives, potatoes, radishes, and spinach) with any of the other vegetables (which are deeper-rooted) so that there is no competition for water and nutrients.

*Interplant corn with scarlet runner beans (BELOW LEFT) to make the most use of space.*

*Peas (BELOW RIGHT) not only provide nutrition for the gardener, they also put nitrogen back in the soil.*

the third planting, use legumes, which fix nitrogen into the soil; these include peas, beans, and peanuts. Never follow a light feeder with a heavy feeder unless the soil is built up again. For this reason, it's a good idea to keep a record of what you plant and when and where you plant it.

Choosing the right varieties to match your environmental conditions is probably more important for vegetables than for any other type of plants. There are varieties of corn, for example, that were bred for northern gardens with short growing seasons and onions designed for growing in the south that will not form bulbs in the north. There are also differences among varieties regarding their disease and insect resistance. If you live in an area with short summers, look at the days to maturity carefully, and make sure there is enough time to harvest those crops that have a long growing season. Your cooperative extension office will probably have a list of the best varieties for your area.

With many vegetables, there are both hybrid and nonhybrid varieties available. The hybrids are more expensive but have better vigor, increased yield, and increased disease resistance. New varieties come onto the market every year, and it is fun to experiment with these. Keep in mind, however, that seeds you may have collected from hybrid varieties planted in your garden will not grow true and should not be used.

© Derek Fell

## ■ GROWING THE VEGETABLE GARDEN

Depending on the particular vegetable, it can be planted into the garden from seeds, from plants, or sometimes from either. These conditions are spelled out in the dictionary. If a vegetable can be grown either way, it's best to start it from plants in areas with short growing seasons. If you're starting your own plants indoors from seed, allow five to seven weeks before planting time, unless otherwise indicated in the dictionary.

Follow all the guidelines in the previous chapters regarding soil preparation, fertilizing, and garden care. The fertilizer incorporated into the soil at planting time will be sufficient for the crop unless otherwise specified in the dictionary. The pH for most vegetables should be 5.5 to 6.8, but where there are exceptions, this is also noted in the dictionary. When growing vegetables, it

*Extend the season (ABOVE LEFT) by planting hardy crops early and protecting* *them from frost when necessary with milk containers.*

*Seedlings are protected from frost with plastic (ABOVE), which can be pulled back during the day to let in sunlight and fresh air.*

is very important to provide ample, deep, and even moisture, never letting the ground become too dry.

Young seedlings are subject to some devastating effects of nature. If a late and unexpected frost threatens, cover your warm-season vegetables with plastic film, plastic cups or other containers, or purchased cloches until it has warmed up. Watch out for snails, slugs, and cutworms, which do most of their damage when plants are young.

If you are growing cool-season vegetables, apply mulch early to keep the ground cool. On the other hand, don't apply mulch until the soil is warm if you are growing warm-season vegetables. Black and clear plastic mulches will trap heat and are a good technique to use when growing warm-season vegetables in cool areas or in areas with short growing seasons because they increase the soil temperature.

For best flavor and texture and to encourage more vegetables on those plants that produce all season, always harvest as soon as the crop is ready. In autumn, remove all annual plants from the garden for appearance's sake as well as to remove overwintering sites for insects and diseases.

Vegetables are excellent candidates for containers. Choose those whose growth habit is naturally compact; attempting to grow pumpkins in a container would be an excercise in futility. There are many vegetables, like tomatoes and cucumbers, that now have "bush" varieties, and these would be better choices for containers than their larger, vining cousins. Potatoes and other root crops can be grown in bushel baskets; at harvest time, the basket can be emptied and the crop removed, eliminating digging. When growing in any type of container, use a very rich soil and pay close attention to watering, which may be needed every day.

# A Dictionary of Vegetables

### *Abelmoschus esculentus*
### Okra

■ Start okra (a warm-season vegetable) from seeds sown outdoors after all danger of frost has passed and the soil is warm. Plant 18 inches (45 cm) apart, and harvest in 55 to 70 days when the pods are 3 to 5 inches (7.5 to 12.5 cm) long. Feed three times during the season for best production. Okra is prone to attack from corn earworms and cabbageworms.

### *Allium cepa*
### Onion

■ Onions (a warm-season vegetable) are divided into two groups based on their sensitivity to day length. Be sure to purchase varieties specific for your area. In mid-spring, plant seedlings started indoors 12 weeks earlier, plant "sets" (tiny bulbs), or sow seeds outdoors. Space 2 to 5 inches (5 to 12.5 cm) apart, harvesting in 75 to 100 days when the tops have fallen over. Feed at planting time and once again during the growing season. Thrips and maggots are common pests, and crop rotation will lessen the chance of such diseases as onion smut.

*Okra*

*Celery*

## *Apium graveolens*
## Celery

■ Start seeds indoors 2 to 4 months before setting plants out in late spring, soaking seeds in hot water before planting to prevent diseases. Celery (a warm-season vegetable) has a growing period of 90 to 130 days and should be planted 6 inches (15cm) apart. Fertilize monthly, and provide plenty of water, never letting the soil become dry.

## *Arachis hypogaea*
## Peanuts

■ The unique growing habit of peanuts (a warm-season vegetable) makes it worth experimentation, but don't try it unless you have a long, hot summer of at least 120 days. Plant seeds after frost danger has passed, and thin to 2 feet (60cm) apart. After the flowers fade, a peg grows downward from the plant into the ground, where the peanuts form. Dig them up after the plant turns yellow at the end of the season, and dry for 2 to 3 weeks. Soil should be slightly alkaline and high in calcium to grow good peanuts; peanuts fix nitrogen in the soil and need only light feeding.

## *Allium sativum*
## Garlic

■ Garlic (a cool-season vegetable) is grown from cloves usually planted in autumn in mild areas and in the early spring in cold areas. Set them 1 inch deep and 2 to 4 inches (5 to 10cm) apart, with the pointed end up. Use a low-nitrogen fertilizer at planting time and again when the tops are 6 inches (15cm) high. Harvest in about 90 days, when the tops turn yellow and fall over.

## *Allium ampeloprasum*
## Leeks

■ Set plants into the garden in early spring, spacing them 3 inches (7.5cm) apart. Fertilize leeks (a warm-season vegetable) at planting time and again when the tops are 6 inches (15cm) high. Harvest in autumn when the stalks are 3 3/4 to 1 1/2 inches (1.9 to 3.75 cm) across.

## *Armoracia rusticana*
### Horseradish

■ A perennial that can be grown as an annual, horseradish (a warm-season vegetable) is started from root cuttings planted in mid-spring. Space 12 inches (30cm) apart, and harvest in 150 days or late autumn.

## *Asparagus officinalis*
### Asparagus

■ A perennial, asparagus (a warm-season vegetable) can be started from seeds but is better started from purchased crowns. It will take 2 to 3 years before it can be harvested annually by cutting the spears off below ground level. Plant 15 inches (37.5 cm) apart. Asparagus likes a very rich soil and should be fertilized when growth starts in spring and again after harvesting. Choose rust-resistant varieties, and be on the watch for asparagus beetles.

## *Beta vulgaris*
### Beet

■ Sow seeds outdoors from mid-spring through midsummer for harvesting within 50 to 70 days when the beets are 2 to 3 inches (5 to 7.5cm) across. Thin to 2 inches (5cm) apart. Beets (a cool-season vegetable) are biennials grown as annuals

because the flesh becomes tough and stringy the second year. Look for varieties resistant to downy mildew if this is a problem in your area. Beet greens are subject to attack by flea beetles and leaf miners; the roots can be attacked by nematodes. Test the pH and keep it above 6.5 and below 8.0.

## *Beta vulgaris*
### Swiss chard

■ Grown for its leaves rather than its roots, Swiss chard is a close relative of the beet. Sow seeds outdoors from mid-spring through midsummer for harvesting in 55 to 65 days. Space 8 inches (20cm) apart. Swiss chard (a warm-season vegetable) is a biennial grown as an annual. It is fairly free of insect and disease problems.

*Cauliflower*

© Joanne Pavia

## *Brassica napus*
### Rutabaga

■ Sow seeds outdoors in early summer for harvesting in cool weather 90 to 120 days later. Thin to 6 to 8 inches (15 to 20cm) apart. Rutabaga (a cool-season vegetable) is grown in the same way as cabbage but is not as prone to insect or disease attack.

## *Brassica oleracea*
### Cabbage and its relatives

■ Cabbage and its relatives (cool-season vegetables) grow best if harvested when temperatures are below 80°F (27°C). Seeds of cabbage, kale, and kohlrabi can be sown outdoors in early spring; those of broccoli and cauliflower are sown outdoors in mid-spring; brussels sprouts are sown in late spring; collards are sown in midsummer. Purchased or indoor-started plants can also be set outdoors: cabbage, kale, and kohlrabi in early spring; broccoli and cauliflower in mid-spring; brussels sprouts in early summer; collards in midsummer. Cabbage,

© Jerry Pavia

*Beets*

broccoli, cauliflower, kale, and kohlrabi can also be set outdoors in summer about 3 to 4 months before the first autumn frost. The following chart outlines the planting distances and the time to harvest.

|  | DAYS TO HARVEST | SPACING |
|---|---|---|
| **Broccoli** | 70–95 | 18 inches (45cm) |
| **Brussels sprouts** | 90–120 | 2 feet (60cm) |
| **Cabbage** | 70–80 | 1 to 2 feet (30 to 60cm) |
| **Cauliflower** | 50–70 | 2 feet (60cm) |
| **Collards** | 70–90 | 15 inches (37.5cm) |
| **Kale** | 60–70 | 9 to 12 inches (22.5 to 30cm) |
| **Kohlrabi** | 50–60 | 6 inches (15cm) |

Feed cabbage and its relatives at planting time and again in 4 weeks. Keeping the pH in the 6.5 to 7.5 range discourages clubroot disease; downy mildew and fusarium wilts are other major diseases. It is wise to rotate cabbage crops with other vegetables every year and look for disease-resistant varieties. Cabbage and its relatives can be attacked by cabbage loopers, cabbageworms, cabbage maggots, aphids, cutworms, flea beetles, and harlequin bugs.

© Charles Mann

## Brassica rapa
### Chinese cabbage, turnip

■ It is surprising to most gardeners that these dissimilar vegetables (both cool-season vegetables) are so closely related. Seeds of Chinese cabbage should be sown outdoors in midsummer for harvesting in 75 days, while those of the turnip are sown outdoors in midsummer for harvesting 70 days after a light frost. Turnips can also be planted in early spring for harvesting before it becomes 80°F (27°C). Bok choy is a close relative of Chinese cabbage and can be used as either a spring or autumn crop, maturing in 45 to 50 days. Thin Chinese cabbage to 1¹/₂ feet (45cm) apart, and turnips to 3 to 5 inches (7.5 to 12.5cm) apart. Rotate plants to prevent diseases. Aphids and flea beetles are the main insect pests of turnips; Chinese cabbage suffers from the same troubles as cabbage.

*Peppers*

## Capsicum annuum
### Pepper, sweet or hot

■ Sow seeds or set plants outdoors after frost danger has passed (both are warm-season vegetables). Plant 1¹/₂ feet (45cm) apart, and harvest in 60 to 80 days. Hot peppers need higher temperatures than sweet bell peppers do. Fertilize at planting time, and feed again lightly when flowers develop. Although peppers have a long list of potential insect and disease troubles, they are usually resistant to damage.

## Cichorium endivia
### Endive, escarole

■ Endive has curled and cut leaves, while escarole has smooth, broad leaves (both are cool-season vegetables). Set plants or sow seeds outdoors in midsummer for harvesting in autumn, 80 to 100 days later. Both can be grown in spring, but tend to be more bitter if they are. Space 8 to 12 inches (20 to 30cm) apart.

## Citrullus lanatus
### Watermelon

■ Set seeds or plants outdoors after all danger of frost has passed and the soil is warm, spacing 4 feet (1.2m) apart. Feed at planting time, when the

*Endive*

runners are 18 inches (45cm) long, and when the fruit sets. Watermelons (a warm-season fruit) will be ready for picking in 75 to 95 days; they require more summer heat than other types of melons. They are also one of the few vegetables that tolerate a soil pH below 6.0. Watermelons are more resistant to insects and diseases than other melons.

## *Cucumis melo*
### Melon (muskmelon and cantaloupe)
■ Plant and grow the same time as watermelon (they are also warm-season fruits), but space 2 to 3 feet (60 to 90cm) apart. In areas with short growing seasons, start with plants. Harvest time is 65 to 110 days, depending on the type and variety. Select disease-resistant varieties, and protect from cucumber beetles and aphids.

## *Cucumis sativus*
### Cucumber
■ Plant or sow outdoors after all danger of frost has passed and the ground is warm. Set 1 to 2 feet (30 to 60cm) apart and harvest in 50 to 75 days. Slicing cucumbers should be 7 to 8 inches (17.5 to 20cm) long, and pickling types 1½ to 3 inches (3.8 to 7.5cm) long. Cucumbers (a warm-season vegetable) favor very rich soil and deep watering and like additional fertilizer at least once during the growing season. Where space is limited, grow on a trellis or other support. Look for disease-resistant varieties, and do not water from overhead if downy mildew is troublesome. Insect pests include aphids, cucumber and flea beetles, and squash bugs.

## *Cucurbita pepo*
### Summer squash

■ After the danger of frost has passed and the ground is warm (summer squash is a warm-season vegetable), set out plants or sow seeds. Space 3 to 4 feet (90cm to 2m) apart in rich, fertile soil, applying a second feeding halfway through the season. Harvest in 50 to 55 days when young and tender. Any member of the squash family is subject to aphids, cucumber beetles, squash bugs, and squash vine borers.

## *Cucurbita* species
### Winter squash

■ Plant or sow winter squash (a warm-season vegetable) outdoors after all danger of frost has passed and the ground is warm. Set 6 to 8 feet (1.8 to 2.4m) apart in rich, fertile soil, refeeding at least once and preferably twice during the season. Harvest 75 to 120 days after the first frost; they will be sweeter this way. Winter squash suffers the same problems as summer squash.

## *Cucurbita* species
### Pumpkin

■ Plant or sow pumpkins (a warm-season plant) and grow in the same way as squash, but allow 3 to 4 feet (90cm to 1.2m) between plants. The best time to harvest is after 90 to 120 days, when the foliage starts to die. Fertilize at planting time and again monthly through the growing season.

## *Daucus carota*
### Carrot

■ Sow carrot seeds outdoors from early spring through early summer (they are cool-season plants), thinning to 1 to 2 inches (2.5 to 5cm) apart. Pull from the ground in 50 to 70 days when they are 2 inches (5cm) or less across; they can be left in the ground all winter, but this will make them less tender. Soil must be very loose and very rich or the carrots will be deformed.

*Pumpkin (RIGHT)*

*Summer squash (LEFT)*

## *Ipomoea batatas*
### Sweet potato

■ This tropical plant (a warm-season vegetable) is the most heat-demanding of any vegetable grown in the United States or Canada; don't even try to grow it unless you have 95 to 125 days where the nights are above 70°F (21°C). Start from cuttings known as "slips"; look for slips certified to be disease free, and plant them 12 inches (30cm) apart. Use a low-nitrogen fertilizer when preparing the soil. Harvest when the plants start to turn yellow, and cure the sweet potatoes in a warm, humid room for 2 weeks.

## *Lactuca sativa*
### Lettuce

■ Lettuce (a cool-season vegetable) is divided into 4 types: leaf, butterhead, Romaine, and iceberg (crisphead). Set plants or sow seeds outdoors in mid-spring for harvest in 45 to 75 days. Plants should be 6 to 12 inches (15 to 30cm) apart. Replant for an autumn crop. Fertilize every 2 weeks with liquid fertilizer. Lettuce can be afflicted with mildew and wilt and is subject to attack by aphids, cabbage loopers, cutworms, flea beetles, leafhoppers, slugs, and snails.

© Lynn Karlin

*© Lynn Karlin*

## *Lycopersicon lysopersicum*
### Tomato

■ Tomatoes (a warm-weather vegetable) are classified as either determinate or indeterminate. The former has fruit that matures at the same time, making them useful for canning. The latter continues to bear fruit all season until frost, making them the best type for salads. Place transplants in the garden in late spring, 2 to 3 feet (60 to 90cm) apart for the bush types and 1½ feet (45cm) apart for the vining types. Bury the stem up to the first leaves to produce stronger plants. Tomatoes will be ready for picking in 60 to 80 days. Feed at planting time, when fruit first sets, and monthly after that. Choosing disease-resistant varieties is essential for successful tomato growing. Tomato hornworms are serious pests but can be controlled. To prevent blossom end rot, keep plants evenly moist. Interplanted with cabbage, tomatoes can repel flea beetles.

## *Pastinaca sativa*
### Parsnip

■ Sow seeds outdoors in mid-spring (parsnips are a warm-season plant); they take a long time to germinate and have poor germination, so sow heavily. Space 2 inches (5cm) apart. Harvest in autumn after the first frost; this improves their flavor. They can also be left in the ground all winter. Parsnips are seldom bothered by insects or diseases.

## *Phaseolus limensis*
### Lima bean

■ Lima beans (a warm-weather vegetable) are designated as either pole or bush. Pole beans grow more slowly than bush types, but produce more beans over a longer period. Sow seeds outdoors in late spring after all danger of frost has passed and the soil is warm. Space pole beans 6 to 10 inches (15 to 25cm) apart, and bush beans 3 to 4 inches (7.5 to 10cm) apart. Harvest in 65 to 90 days. Lima beans need a longer and hotter growing season than green beans. With both types, diseases can be prevented by rotating crops every year and by not working in the garden when the foliage is wet. Mexican bean beetles and leafhoppers are the primary insect pests of beans. Beans fix nitrogen in the soil and therefore need only light feeding.

© Lynn Karlin

## Phaseolus vulgaris
### Green bean

■ Like lima beans, green beans (also a warm-season vegetable) are either pole or bush. Sow seeds outdoors in late spring after all danger of frost has passed and the soil is warm. Grow in the same manner as lima beans. Bush beans can be harvested in 50 to 70 days; pole beans take longer —60 to 90 days.

## Pisum sativum
### Pea

■ Sow seeds outdoors in early spring as soon as the soil can be worked. Peas (a cool-season vegetable) can also be planted in autumn in warm areas. Thin to 1 to 2 inches (2.5 to 5cm) apart; vining types will need to be trained on a trellis. Peas can be picked in 55 to 70 days. To discourage diseases, avoid overhead watering; also look for disease-resistant varieties. Aphids and thrips are the most common insects that attack peas.

## Raphanus sativus
### Radish

■ Sow seeds outdoors as soon as the ground can be worked in early spring (radishes are a cool-season vegetable), and sow successively until warm weather sets in. Thin to 1 inch (2.5cm) apart, and harvest in 21 to 35 days. Fertilize at planting time, and apply liquid fertilizer two weeks after germination. Maggots and flea beetles can bother radishes but diseases are rarely a problem. Interplanted with cucumbers, radishes can repel cucumber beetles.

*Rhubarb (BELOW)*

## *Rheum rhabarbarum*
## Rhubarb

■ Rhubarb can be grown only where there is at least 2 months of frost, a long, cool spring, and summers under 90°F (32°C) (making it a warm- and cool-season plant). Start with rooted crowns, planting them 12 inches (30cm) deep and 3 feet (90cm) apart. Do not harvest the first year, but after that, harvest up to half the stalks at any one time, cutting them in late spring. Fertilize this perennial in early spring and again after harvesting. Always cook rhubarb, and eat only the stalks, as the leaves are poisonous.

## *Solanum melongena*
## Eggplant

■ Add seeds or plants to the garden in late spring after all danger of frost has passed and the air and ground are warm (eggplant is a warm-season vegetable). Space 1½ to 2 feet (45 to 60cm) apart, and harvest in 75 to 95 days from plants and 150 days from seed, when fruit is 3 to 4 inches (7.5 to 10cm) long. Feed at planting time, and once a month after that. Flea, cucumber, and Colorado potato beetles are particular nuisances.

## *Solanum tuberosum*
## Potato

■ Although you can grow potatoes (a warm-season vegetable) from your own "eyes," it is better to purchase certified "eyes" as these will be disease-free. Plant 4 inches (10cm) deep and 12 inches (30cm) apart in rich, fertile, sandy soil in mid-spring; harvest in autumn about 120 days later when the vines have turned yellow. Keep the pH between 4.8 and 5.4 to prevent scab disease; also look for disease-resistant varieties. Colorado potato beetles, flea beetles, and leafhoppers are the chief insect pests. Keep soil mounded up around the base of the plants to keep the potatoes from turning green and becoming inedible.

© Lynn Karlin

*Spinach*

© Lynn Karlin

## *Spinacia oleracea*
### Spinach

■ Sow seeds outdoors in early spring as soon as the soil can be worked, and sow again in autumn about a month and a half before the first frost (spinach is a cool-season vegetable). Thin to 3 to 6 inches (7.5 to 15 cm). Harvest in 45 to 55 days, in spring before the weather becomes hot and the plants bolt to seed. Select bolt-resistant varieties for spring planting; also select disease-resistant varieties. Cabbage loopers, cucumber beetles, leaf miners, and leafhoppers can attack but are not a serious problem if growing is limited to cool weather.

## *Tetragonia tetragonoides*
### New Zealand spinach

■ This is a good substitute for spinach in areas where it is too warm to grow spinach (New Zealand spinach is a warm-season vegetable). Sow seeds outdoors in late spring, thinning to 1¹/₂ feet (45 cm) apart. Leaves will be ready for harvest in 60 to 90 days.

## *Zea mays*
### Corn

■ Sow seeds outdoors in late spring (corn is a warm-season vegetable), thinning to 1 foot (30 cm) apart. For best pollination, plant corn in squares rather than in long rows. Harvest after 60 to 90 days when the silk becomes dry and brown. Look for one of the new supersweet varieties for more mouth-watering flavor than the standard varieties. For a continuous supply, plant varieties with different days to maturity or make successive plantings every two to three weeks. Fertilize at planting time, and again when plants are 8 inches (20 cm) high and 18 inches (45 cm) high. Look for varieties resistant to corn earworms; also treat the silks with BT when they form.

*Chapter Seven*

# THE NATURAL HERB GARDEN

© Amla Sanghvi

*Fill up all of your senses (BELOW) with a variety of herbs.*

*Many herbs, such as catnip (RIGHT), can be grown as a garden ornamental as well as for use in the kitchen.*

*Fill up all of your senses (BELOW) with a variety of herbs.*

© Charles Mann

Whether you pronounce it "urb" or "hurb," herbs have been treasured by gardeners since ancient times for their aroma, uses, dependability, insect-repelling qualities, and the legends attached to them, perhaps more so than any other class of plant. The term "herb" refers to any plant that is valued for its flavorful, aromatic, or medicinal qualities. Herbs are used as seasonings in cooking (imparting flavor without salt), in drinks, as garnishes, as dried flowers, in cosmetics and soaps, in potpourri, as dyes, and to repel insects. Beekeepers often plant herbs whose flowers attract bees.

Depending on the plant, an herb may be an annual, a biennial, or a perennial. Also depending on the plant, the leaves, flowers, seeds, roots, or stems are harvested for use.

Annual herbs are categorized as hardy or tender. Hardy annuals will withstand light frost and can be planted in early spring or in autumn and overwintered; tender annuals are killed by frost and cannot be planted until all danger of frost has passed in spring. Some herbs that are perennials in warm climates may be grown as annuals in colder areas. Some herbs that are biennials can also be grown as annuals. In the following herb dictionary, you will find out each herb's category and, if it is a perennial or biennial, its hardiness zones.

There are two considerations when selecting herbs for the garden: matching the environment and growing conditions in your garden with the right plants and choosing plants for their visual impact and desired uses.

Herbs have definite climatic preferences. Some herbs prefer cool growing conditions, while others must have hot weather. Each biennial and perennial herb has a range of hardiness zones in which it will grow; there is a minimum winter temperature each will endure, and some must have freezing temperatures in winter to grow well (check the hardiness zone map on page 186). Herbs also have preferences for sun or shade, and although most prefer dry soil, some need moist soil conditions. The dictionary outlines the environmental needs for the most popular herbs. Study this section carefully before selecting the herbs to grow in your garden.

Once you have matched plants to your growing conditions and decided whether you want to grow annuals or perennials or a mixture of both, select herbs that are the size, shape, and flower color of your liking, because many are attractive garden plants. Also select those herbs that you would like to use in cooking, teas, potpourri, dried flower arrangements, or for other uses.

*Herbs such as parsley (BELOW) can be interplanted with such vegetables as chard.*

*The knot garden (RIGHT) is the most traditional way to design an herb garden.*

## ■ DESIGNING WITH HERBS

If you have the space, a garden devoted entirely to herbs can be easily designed. Traditional designs include knot gardens and wagon wheels. If you are designing one of these, choose herbs that are low-growing, compact, and easily clipped. Using plants with contrasting textures or colors is most dramatic.

However, herbs can also be planted in beds and borders like other garden plants. Herbs can be mixed into flower beds and borders, integrated into vegetable gardens, grown in pots, grown as edgings or ground

covers, or grown in rock gardens, depending on their size and growth habit. If you are growing only culinary herbs, placing them near the kitchen door allows you to quickly go outside and snip a few leaves as needed.

Most herbs are delightfully fragrant and can be used near outdoor living spaces or open windows. Many have gray or colored foliage that can be used to accent or buffer other plants. Caraway and dill have attractive, finely cut foliage that makes a nice contrast to coarser plants such as angelica and borage. Lower-growing thyme and mint can be used as ground covers. Basil, chives, marjoram, and parsley can be grown indoors on a windowsill.

Many gardeners like to plant herbs in "theme" gardens; plants to make teas, for example, or fragrant plants or plants for dried flowers.

## ■ GROWING HERBS NATURALLY

Herbs are among the easiest plants to grow naturally, because they require little care and have very few insect and disease problems.

Depending on the plant, herbs are propagated by seeds, cuttings, or division. If an herb can be propagated by seed, you can start your own seeds indoors in early spring or direct-sow them into the garden, depending on the plant. Cumin, lemon balm, rosemary, and savory should be started indoors; borage and caraway should be started in the garden. Others can be seeded as desired. Keep in mind that anise, borage, caraway, chervil, coriander, cumin, dill, fennel, lovage, parsley, and savory resent transplanting. If you are not sowing them directly into the ground, start them indoors in individual pots to lessen transplanting shock. Also reread the section in chapter three on starting plants from seed.

© Lynn Karlin

Some annual herbs and almost every perennial herb can be propagated by cuttings; techniques for doing this are outlined in chapter three. Most perennial herbs will need dividing either when they stop growing well, when they become too large, or when the center dies out. The divisions can be used to propagate new plants or to share your herb garden with neighbors and friends. For instructions on how to divide herbs, see chapter three.

If you do not wish to propagate your own herbs, you can buy plants at the garden center or from mail-order catalogs in spring. Select plants that are healthy in appearance and preferably not in bloom; if it is an herb you plan to use for cooking, smell or taste a little piece of the leaf to make sure you like the aroma or flavor. Be sure to water plants regularly until planting time.

Planting time for herbs depends on the type of plant. Hardy annuals can be planted as soon as the soil can be worked in early to mid-spring, which is about four weeks before the last frost. Those herbs that are tender annuals cannot be planted until all danger of frost has passed in the spring. Which category each particular herb fits into is specified in the dictionary. Perennials and biennials can be added to the garden any time from mid-spring until approximately six weeks before the first autumn frost, unless they are being grown as annuals, in

*Herbs and flowers (LEFT)
make a perfect pair in
garden spaces.*

*Sweet woodruff (BELOW) is
home in rich, acid, moist
soil. Other herbs prefer
drier and poorer conditions.*

which case they are planted in spring. Planting distances are outlined in the dictionary.

For every rule there must be an exception, and so it is with herbs. Herbs vary in their need for rich or only slightly rich, fertile or only slightly fertile soil. Too much organic matter and/or fertilizer can ruin the flavor of some herbs or cause others to grow too much foliage at the expense of flowers and seeds. If an herb needs slightly rich soil (as specified in the dictionary), add minimal organic matter when preparing the soil. If it needs rich soil, be extra generous with organic matter. Otherwise, prepare the soil in the normal manner as outlined in chapter one.

If an herb likes slightly fertile soil, add only a small amount of fertilizer at planting time. Otherwise, incorporate the normal amount of balanced fertilizer into the soil before planting; no further feeding will usually be necessary during the growing season. As long as they don't prefer slightly fertile soil, feed biennial and perennial herbs again each year when growth begins; those that prefer slightly fertile soil may not need feeding for several years, depending on their growth.

Many herbs like dry soil; soil that's too wet can ruin their flavor or aroma or cause them to rot. Herbs with average moisture requirements should receive 1 inch (2.5cm) of water per week; the soil surface should never dry out if an herb prefers moist soil. The moisture requirements for each herb are specified in the dictionary.

The ideal pH for most herbs is 6.5 to 7.0. Basil, borage, burnet, caraway, chervil, coriander, cumin, fennel, hyssop, lavender, lavender cotton, lemon balm, lovage, marjoram, mint, parsley, thyme, rosemary, rue, sage, savory, and tarragon will grow in slightly alkaline soil. Angelica, basil, borage, catnip, dill, lemon balm,

lemon verbena, lovage, rosemary, rue, sage, scented geraniums, tansy, and thyme will tolerate slightly acid soils. Sweet woodruff must be grown at a pH of 4.5 to 5.5.

If an herb is growing too tall and lanky, pinch out the central growing tip to keep it compact and bushy. If an herb is being grown for its foliage, remove flower buds as they form to keep the leaves productive and more flavorful. If an herb is not being grown for its flowers and/or seeds, cut it back during midsummer if it gets too spindly. Some herbs are invasive growers, and these can be kept in check by removing flowers before they drop seeds or by installing edgings of metal or stone as barriers.

If an herb prefers cool growing conditions, mulch it as early as possible in the spring to keep the ground cool. If, on the other hand, warm conditions are preferred, apply mulch in late spring after the ground has warmed up.

*Tie up bunches of herbs (BELOW) to dry in a well-ventilated attic.*

Taller herbs may need staking. Growing weak-stemmed plants, such as dill, close together will also allow the plants to prop each other up.

Perennial herbs may need winter protection if grown near their hardiness limit (see chapter three). Some herbs, such as lavender, sage, tarragon, and thyme, are more damaged by poorly drained soil during the winter than they are by cold weather; improve drainage if you encounter this problem by improving the soil or by building raised beds.

In autumn, after they are killed by frost, annual herbs should be removed from the beds and perennial herbs cut to the ground. This is for visual appearance as well as to remove breeding sites for insects and diseases.

Most herbs are relatively problem free when it comes to insect and disease problems (in fact, many are insect-repelling), but be on the lookout for damage.

## ■ HARVESTING AND DRYING HERBS

Throughout the growing season, it's a delight to be able to snip fresh herbs to use in the kitchen. After the season has faded, dried leaves, flowers, and other plant parts can be put to use to extend the enjoyment of the herb garden throughout the year.

Fresh herb leaves have more flavor than dried leaves and are usually most flavorful before the plants bloom. Harvest leaves for fresh or dried use any time they are large enough, cutting them off on a dry, sunny morning after the dew has dried. If cutting flowers for drying, pick them when they are one third to two thirds open and not wet from dew or rain.

Several weeks after the flowers in the garden have faded, seeds will be ready for harvest; they often change color to tan or gray at this point. There are two ways to harvest seeds. The first is to knock them from the faded

© Lynn Karlin

*A dried herb wreath (RIGHT) extends the life of the herb garden.*

flowers into a paper bag. The second is to cut the stems with the faded flowers and hang them indoors, upside down in a paper bag, so the seeds will fall into the bag. Cut stems or dig roots that have herbal uses at the end of the growing season.

Herb leaves can be dried by first washing and blotting them dry and then by hanging the stems upside down in a dry, dark, well-ventilated spot. If the stems are short or individual leaves are being dried, dry them on a drying rack or a screen. This will take about two weeks. Herbs can also be dried on cookie sheets in a gas oven that has a pilot light; the process will take about three days. In an electric oven set on the lowest temperature, herbs will dry in a few hours. You can also experiment with drying leaves in a microwave. Basil, burnet, chervil, chives, and fennel do not air dry well and are best frozen; parsley is best dried in the refrigerator. Leaves should be removed from the stems when dry and stored whole.

It is also possible to preserve the flavor of herbs by mixing them with vinegar, butter, cream cheese, sour cream, or mayonnaise, or by using them to make jellies.

Most herb flowers that can be dried can be air dried. After cutting them, strip the leaves from the stems and tie the stems together in small bunches. Hang them upside down in a dark, airy room that is not too hot. They will be ready in two to three weeks. Flowers with thin stems should have florists' wire wrapped around the stems before drying; these can be air dried head up in a coffee can or other container. After the flowers are dried, they can be used in a variety of ways, including arrangements, wreaths, and pictures, or in potpourri.

Seeds may be dry enough as they fall from the faded flowers. If not, spread them on a screen or piece of cheesecloth to dry.

Most flowers, leaves, and seeds that have been dried will absorb moisture in a humid room. You should therefore store them in an airtight container when they are not in use. If moisture collects inside the container, they need further drying. Do not store herbs near the heat from the stove or in the sunshine as this will accelerate their loss of flavor. It is also best to store them in dark bottles to keep the light from them.

Potpourri is a mixture of dried flowers, leaves, essential oils, spices, and a fixative that retains its fragrance for many years. Although rose petals are traditional in making potpourri, any other fragrant petals or leaves can be used, and many herbs are perfect for this. To make dry potpourri, dry petals or leaves on a screen until crisp. To each quart of dried material, add 1 ounce (30ml) of orrisroot or other fixative, which will make the scent of the mixture permanent. Add spices such as cloves or cinnamon and a few drops of essential oil, which can be purchased. Mix together well and store in an airtight jar.

Wet potpourri, which holds its scent longer than dry potpourri, is made with partially dried petals or leaves. Alternate layers of petals or leaves with a sprinkling of table salt in a nonmetallic container until it is full. Add fixative, spices, and essential oil, and place a weight on the mixture for several weeks, then mix.

# 🌿 A Dictionary of Herbs 🌿

Below are outlined the descriptions and growing requirements for the most popular herbs. They are listed in alphabetical order by their Latin name, followed by their common name. Next are the light, temperature, and soil moisture requirements, and the hardiness rating. Lastly, there is a description of the plant and any special care needs.

If a plant is listed as needing full sun, it needs at least 6 hours of sun a day. Partial shade is 4 to 6 hours of sun a day, and shade is less than 4 hours of sun. Cool temperatures are below 70°F (21°C), average temperatures are 70°F to 85°F (21°C to 30°C), and hot temperatures are over 85°F (30°C). If a plant needs dry soil, allow the top inch of soil to become dry before watering. If a plant has average water requirements, water when the soil surface becomes dry. When moist soil is needed, never let the soil surface dry out. An annual's hardiness rating falls into one of three categories: tender (plants should not be planted until all danger of frost is gone and the ground is warm, and they will die with the first frost of autumn); half-hardy (plants will not survive frost but can be planted during the cool weather of early spring); and hardy (plants will withstand some frost and can be planted in late fall or early spring). Compare the zones listed with the hardiness zone map on page 186.

*Chives*

## *Allium schoenoprasum*
Chives

- *Sun; average temperatures; moist soil; zones 3–10*
- Globes of purple flowers bloom in mid-spring over 8- to 12-inch (20 to 30cm) tufts of grassy leaves; both the flowers and the leaves can be used in cooking to impart a mild onion flavor. Grow from seeds or divisions set 6 to 8 inches (15 to 20cm) apart in rich soil. Chives repel aphids and mites and help keep rabbits out of the vegetable garden.

© Charles Mann

© Charles Mann

*Dill*

## Anethum graveolens
Dill

- *Sun; average temperatures; moist soil; hardy annual*
- Flat heads of yellow flowers bloom in midsummer atop 2- to 3-foot (60 to 90cm) plants with finely cut foliage. Both the leaves and the seeds are harvested—seeds for pickling and leaves for flavoring. Grow from seeds and thin plants to stand 6 to 10 inches (15 to 25cm) apart so they can support each other. Interplanted with tomatoes, dill repels the tomato hornworm. Don't plant dill near fennel or the two will cross-pollinate and the seeds will not be usable.

## Angelica archangelica
Angelica

- *Sun; hot temperatures; moist soil; zones 4–8*
- Bold, aromatic leaves clothe 5-foot (1.5m) plants topped with clusters of greenish white flowers in the early summer of their second year. Start from seeds sown after they have been refrigerated for six weeks, and set plants 3 feet (90cm) apart. The leaves, stems, seeds, and roots can be used in cooking, and the stems and leafstalks are often candied; all have a mild licorice flavor. Angelica is a biennial but can be grown as an annual; if grown as a biennial, it reseeds easily.

## Aloysia triphylla
Lemon verbena

- *Sun; average temperatures; moist soil; zones 9–11*
- Where it is too cold to grow lemon verbena as a perennial, it can be grown as an annual. It must be grown from plants or cuttings, which should be set 2 to 5 feet (60cm to 1.5m) apart in rich soil. Plants grow 3 feet (90cm) tall and have white or purple flowers in late summer; the leaves are used to give a lemony accent to drinks or potpourri.

## *Anthriscus cerefolium*
### Chervil

■ *Partial shade to shade; cool temperatures; moist soil, hardy annual*

■ Grown from seed and set 6 to 8 inches (15 to 20cm) apart in rich soil, chervil grows 2 feet (60cm) tall and has flat clusters of white flowers in mid-spring. Sow seeds in individual pots as chervil resents transplanting. Harvest the leaves for cooking; they have a slight licorice flavor.

## *Artemisia dracunculus* var. *sativa*
### French tarragon

■ *Sun; average temperatures; average soil; zones 5–8*

■ French tarragon must be grown from purchased plants or cuttings because it rarely blooms, and even when it does, it does not usually set seed. Space plants 1 to 2 feet (30 to 60cm) apart in rich soil; they grow 3 feet (90cm) tall. Tarragon responds best to fertilizing with fish emulsion. Cut the leaves to use in cooking for their delicate licorice flavor.

## *Borago officinalis*
### Borage

■ *Sun; average temperatures; dry soil; hardy annual*

■ Borage has pretty blue flowers that bloom all summer on 2- to 3-foot (60 to 90cm) plants. Start from plants or seed, spacing 12 inches (30cm) apart. Young leaves (mature leaves are coarse and not pleasant to eat) are used in salads, and flowers can be candied or floated on cold drinks for a cooling garnish. Both taste a little like cucumbers. Borage must be grown in a slightly rich, slightly fertile soil and does not like to be transplanted. Pinch plants when they are 6 inches (15cm) tall to encourage bushiness. Interplanted with tomatoes, borage repels the tomato hornworm. Attractive to bees.

*Coriander*

*Caraway*

## *Carum carvi*
### Caraway

- *Sun; average temperatures; dry soil; zones 3–11*
- Well known for its seeds that top bread and rolls, caraway also has lacy leaves that can be used in salads and roots that can be used in cooking. Grow from plants or seeds spaced 6 to 9 inches (15 to 22.5cm) apart. Plants reach 2 to 2½ feet (60 to 75cm) in height and have flat clusters of white flowers all summer in their second season. Caraway is technically a biennial but is often grown as an annual if planted or sown in autumn.

## *Chamaemelum nobile*
### Russian chamomile

- *Sun; cool temperatures; dry to moist soil; zones 4–9*
- Hugging the ground with lacy, gray-green foliage and growing only 6 inches (15cm) high, Russian chamomile has tiny, white, daisylike flowers that bloom in late summer and are used in tea, as a hair

rinse, or for medicinal purposes. Start from plants or seeds sown at 55°F (13°C) and space 3 to 4 inches (7.5 to 10cm) apart, growing in slightly rich soil. It can be mowed in early spring.

## *Coriandrum sativum*
### Coriander

- *Sun; average temperatures; moist soil; hardy annual*
- The seeds of coriander are lemon scented and used in a variety of international dishes; the leaves taste like a cross between sage and citrus and are sometimes called cilantro. Grow from seeds or purchased plants, spacing 8 to 10 inches apart. Plants grow 2½ feet (75cm) tall and have white or pink flowers in late summer. Coriander repels aphids and Colorado potato beetles.

## *Cuminum cyminum*
### Cumin

- *Sun; hot temperatures; average soil; tender annual*
- Flat clusters of white or rose flowers bloom all summer on 6-inch (15cm) plants with threadlike leaves; the seeds are harvested for culinary uses in a number of international dishes. Start from plants or seeds, spacing 6 inches (15cm) apart. If you don't have 3 months of hot weather, don't even bother trying to grow cumin.

© Lynn Karlin

## *Foeniculum vulgare*
Fennel

■ *Sun; average temperatures; dry to moist soil; zones 9–11*

■ Although perennial in warm climates, fennel is grown in most areas as an annual. It resembles dill, with finely cut, bright green leaves. Plants grow 4 to 5 feet (1.2 to 1.5m) high and have flat clusters of yellow flowers all summer. The leaves, stems, and seeds are used in cooking to impart an anise flavor; use fresh leaves only as dried leaves lose their flavor. Start from seeds or plants spaced 8 to 10 inches (20 to 25cm) apart. Fennel is said to impair the growth of bush beans, caraway, tomatoes, and kohlrabi.

## *Galium odoratum*
Sweet woodruff

■ *Partial shade to shade; average temperatures; moist soil; zones 4–9*

■ Needing a rich but slightly fertile and acidic soil, sweet woodruff (formerly known as *Asperula odorata*) grows 6 to 8 inches (15 to 20cm) high and has white, star-shaped flowers in late spring. Grow from plants or cuttings, and space 12 to 15 inches (30 to 37.5cm) apart. The leaves, which have a clover aroma when dried, are the magical ingredient in May wine and are also used in potpourri.

## *Hysoppus officinalis*
Hyssop

■ *Sun; average temperatures; dry soil; zones 3–7*

■ Grown from seeds, plants, or cuttings and planted 18 to 24 inches (45 to 60cm) apart, hyssop grows into an 18- to 24-inch (45 to 60cm) hedge or border plant with aromatic, dark green leaves. It has violet flowers in early summer that attract bees. Both the leaves and the flowers are used to flavor drinks and have been believed to have medicinal purposes.

*Lavender*

*Chamomile*

## *Lavandula angustifolia*
Lavender

■ *Sun; average temperatures; dry soil; zones 5–9*
■ One of the prettiest plants for an herb garden, lavender grows 18 to 24 inches (45 to 60cm) tall and has gray-green aromatic leaves and fragrant violet to purple flowers that bloom all summer. Start from seeds, cuttings, or plants, and space 12 inches (30cm) apart. The flowers are used in cooking, potpourri, soaps, and lotions; they also attract bees. Lavender grows best in slightly fertile soil.

## *Levisticum officinale*
Lovage

■ *Sun; average temperatures; moist soil; zones 3–8*
■ This 3-foot (90cm) perennial has yellow flowers that bloom all summer and attract bees. It looks like a large celery plant and has many of the same uses as celery. The leaves, seeds, and stems are all used in cooking to impart a celery flavor. Grow from seeds or plants spaced 12 to 15 inches (30 to 37.5cm) apart in rich soil.

## *Matricaria recutita*
Sweet false chamomile

■ *Sun; cool temperatures; dry to moist soil; hardy annual*
■ Unlike Russian chamomile, this plant is an annual that grows 24 to 30 inches (60 to 75cm) tall. Start from seeds spaced 8 inches (20cm) apart, and pick the tiny, white, daisylike flowers that bloom all summer to make teas thought to have medicinal purposes. The foliage has an apple scent and can also be used to brew tea. Slightly rich soil is preferred.

## *Melissa officinalis*
### Lemon balm

■ *Shade to partial shade; average temperatures; dry to moist soil; zones 4–8*

■ Grown from seeds, plants, or cuttings and spaced 18 inches (45cm) apart in slightly rich soil, lemon balm is 2 feet (60cm) tall and has white flowers that bloom all summer and attract bees. The leaves are used in drinks, jelly, and cooked dishes to give a lemony flavor; rubbing fresh leaves on furniture makes a fine polish. It does not grow well where humidity is high.

## *Mentha* species
### Mint

■ *Sun to partial shade; average temperatures; average to moist soil; zones 3–11*

■ There are a number of different mints, all growing 12 to 18 inches (30 to 45cm) high and spreading quickly in the garden. Purple flowers appear in midsummer. Grow from seeds, plants, or cuttings, and space 12 to 24 inches (30 to 60cm) apart in rich soil; purchased plants or cuttings are often better than seeds because the seeds of some mints do not produce flavorful plants. Leaves are harvested for use in a number of recipes and as a garnish for cold summer drinks. Mint can be invasive in the garden. It is a good repellent of cabbage maggots, cabbage moth, flea beetles, and mice.

## *Monarda didyma*
### Bee balm

■ *Sun to partial shade; average temperatures; dry to average soil; zones 4–8*

■ As the name implies, bee balm attracts hundreds of these flying creatures into the garden. Plants grow 2 to 4 feet (60cm to 1.2m) tall and have flowers in a variety of colors, mostly red, pink, or white, which bloom in early to midsummer. Start from seeds, plants, or cuttings, and space 12 inches (30cm) apart. The hairy, somewhat coarse leaves are used to flavor drinks with a mild citrus or minty taste. Bee balm grows best in a slightly fertile and slightly rich soil; it can become invasive, however, and an edging or barrier will prevent it from encroaching onto other plants.

*Bee balm (LEFT)*

*Basil (BELOW)*

## Nasturtium officinale
### Watercress

- *Shade; cool temperatures; moist soil; zones 6–10*
- Watercress likes constant moisture and grows best along streams or other running water. Plants grow 3 inches (7.5cm) high and have round, divided leaves and yellow flowers that bloom in late spring. Grow from seeds or plants spaced 12 to 15 inches (30 to 37.5cm) apart, and pick the leaves to give a peppery taste to salads or as a garnish.

## Nepeta cataria
### Catnip

- *Shade to partial shade; average temperatures; dry soil; zones 3–10*
- Besides giving your cat a delight, the leaves can be used by you to flavor drinks. Grown from seeds or plants spaced 18 to 24 inches (45 to 60cm) apart, catnip is 2 to 4 feet (60cm to 1.2m) tall and has violet flowers in early summer. To keep cats out of young beds, grow catnip from seeds instead of plants, as the oil that attracts cats will be released during planting. Catnip repels a number of insects: cabbage moth, Colorado potato beetle, cucumber beetle, and flea beetle. Catmint is a close relative grown in the same way; both prefer slightly rich and slightly fertile soil.

## Ocimum basilicum
### Basil

- *Sun; average temperatures; average soil; tender annual*
- Start with seeds or plants spaced 10 to 12 inches (25 to 30cm) apart, and enjoy the 18- to 24-inch (45 to 60cm) plants with spikes of white or purple flowers that bloom all summer. Basil, with its green or purple leaves, is ornamental as well as useful. Pinch plants when they are 4 to 6 inches (10 to 15cm) tall to encourage bushiness. No Italian kitchen would be without fresh or dried basil leaves.

© Lynn Karlin

© Jerry Pavia

*Oregano*

## *Origanum* species
### Oregano

■ *Sun; average temperatures; average soil; zones 5–9*
■ Although you can buy oregano seeds, it is better to start with cuttings or plants, since oregano grown from seed often does not have good flavor. Set plants 12 inches apart. White, pink, or purple flowers bloom on 18- to 24-inch (45 to 60cm) plants in midsummer. Oregano leaves are about as indispensable in Italian cooking as basil. Oregano can be grown as an annual and prefers slightly rich and slightly fertile soil.

*Oregano*

## *Origanum majorana*
### Sweet marjoram

■ *Sun; average temperatures; average soil; zones 9-11*
■ A perennial in warm climates, sweet marjoram is usually grown as an annual, and its velvety, aromatic leaves are used in salads or cooked dishes. Start with seeds or plants spaced 6 to 8 inches (15 to 20cm) apart; plants grow 8 to 10 inches high and have inconspicuous clusters of pink flowers in midsummer.

## *Pelargonium* species
### Scented geranium

■ *Sun; average temperatures; average soil; zones 3–10*
■ Depending on the species, scented geraniums can be annuals or perennials; many are perennials only in warm climates and are therefore grown as annuals in most gardens. They also have a wide range of scented leaves—rose, nutmeg, lemon, mint, apple, almond—that can be used in cooked dishes and drinks. Also depending on the species, plants grow anywhere from 1 to 4 feet (30cm to 1.2m) tall, are spaced 1 to 2 feet (30 to 60cm) apart, and have loose clusters of white, pink, or purple flowers that can bloom from late spring through autumn. Grow from seeds or plants; keep in mind that germination is slow and plants are slow to develop from seeds.

*Parsley*

## *Petroselinum crispum*
### Parsley

■ *Shade to partial shade; average temperatures; average soil; zones 3–10*

■ Although parsley is a biennial, it is usually grown as an annual for better flavor. If allowed to grow into its second year, it has yellow-green flowers that bloom in late spring. Plants grow 8 to 12 inches (20 to 30cm) high and have flat or curly leaves used in cooking and as garnishes. Start with seeds or plants spaced 6 to 8 inches (15 to 20cm) apart in rich soil; it is, however, very slow to germinate.

## *Pimpinella anisum*
Anise

■ *Sun; average temperatures; dry soil; hardy annual*

■ The small, lacy leaves and the seeds of anise are used to give a licorice flavor to food and drink and to freshen the breath. Grow from seeds or plants spaced 6 to 9 inches (15 to 22.5 cm) apart. Plants grow 18 to 24 inches (45 to 60cm) high and have flat heads of yellowish white flowers in early summer. Stems are weak; staking them or mounding soil at their base will give them support. Interplanted with vegetables, anise repels aphids and cabbage worm.

## *Poterium sanguisorba*
Burnet

■ *Sun; average temperatures; dry soil; zones 3–10*

■ This perennial likes slightly rich, slightly fertile, and slightly alkaline soil. Its leaves are used in salads and drinks and have a cucumber flavor (leaves must be used fresh, frozen, or stored in vinegar to retain their flavor). Grow from seeds or plants set 15 inches (37.5cm) apart; plants grow 18 to 24 inches (45 to 60cm) tall and have dense tufts of white or pink flowers in early and midsummer.

*Sage*

## *Rosmarinus officinalis*
Rosemary

- *Sun to partial shade; average temperatures; average soil; zones 8–10*
- Where rosemary cannot be grown as a perennial, it can be grown as an annual. Where perennial, light blue flowers bloom on 1- to 5-foot (30cm to 1.5m) plants in early spring. Rosemary can be grown from seeds, plants, or cuttings, and should be spaced 12 to 18 inches (30 to 45cm) apart. The needlelike leaves are used in cooking and sometimes in cosmetics. Rosemary repels cabbage maggots and Mexican bean beetles.

## *Ruta graveolens*
Rue

- *Sun; average temperatures; moist soil; zones 4–10*
- Best grown in slightly rich soil, rue is 18 to 36 inches (45 to 90cm) high and has deeply cut, fernlike blue-green foliage and yellow flowers that bloom in midsummer. Grow from seeds, plants, or cuttings, and space 6 to 12 inches (15 to 30cm) apart. Rue has no culinary uses but is a pretty plant and an excellent insect repellent, especially against Japanese beetles. Wear gloves when handling fresh leaves as they can cause a rash.

*Lavender cotton*

## *Salvia officinalis*
Sage

- *Sun; average temperatures; average to moist soil; zones 3–9*
- Poultry dishes and sausages are a natural match for sage leaves. Grown from seeds, plants, or cuttings and spaced 12 to 18 inches (30 to 45cm) apart, sage grows 18 to 24 inches (45 to 60cm) high and has violet or pink flowers in early summer. Sage repels cabbage maggots and cabbage moths.

## *Santolina chamaecyparissus*
Lavender cotton

- *Sun; average temperatures; dry soil; zones 6–9*
- Lavender cotton is usually used in the herb garden as an edging and insect repellent. Its leaves can also be used in potpourri. It likes slightly rich soil and should be spaced 18 inches (45cm) apart, started from seeds, plants, or cuttings. Although grown for its aromatic, woolly, silver-gray foliage, lavender cotton has yellow flowers that appear in late summer. Where it is cold, it can be grown as an annual. A close relative, *S. virens*, is similar but has green leaves.

### *Satureja hortensis*
### Summer savory

■ *Sun; average temperatures; moist soil; hardy annual*

■ Preferring slightly rich soil, summer savory has loose spikes of lilac, pink, or white flowers that bloom on bushy 12 to 18 inch (30 to 45cm) plants all summer. Start from seeds and space 4 to 6 inches (10 to 15cm) apart; sow successively to have a continual supply all summer. Snip the leaves to use in cooking to impart a delicate peppery flavor or to cut the cooking odor of strong-smelling vegetables like cabbage and turnips. Summer savory is also used to repel Mexican bean beetles.

### *Satureja montana*
### Winter savory

■ *Sun; average temperatures; moist soil; zones 4–9*

■ Like summer savory, winter savory likes slightly rich soil, but it is lower-growing, only 6 to 12 inches (15 to 30cm) high. It is a spreading plant and should be spaced 12 to 15 inches (30 to 37.5cm) apart. Start with seeds or plants. Pink or white flowers bloom in late summer. The leaves are used in the same manner as summer savory but have a stronger flavor.

*Tansy*

© Charles Mann

## *Tanacetum vulgare*
Tansy

■ *Sun; average temperatures; moist soil; zones 3–10*

■ Although the leaves are used in potpourri and the yellow, late-summer flowers can be dried for winter decorations, tansy's best asset is its insect-repelling qualities. It wards off ants, aphids, borers, Colorado potato beetles, cucumber beetles, cutworms, Japanese beetles, and squash bugs; when dried, it is also a good insect repellent for the home. Plants grow 4 feet (1.2 m) tall and should be spaced 12 to 18 inches (30 to 45 cm) apart in rich soil. Grow from seeds or plants.

## *Thymus vulgaris*
Thyme

■ *Sun; average temperatures; dry soil; zones 4–9*

■ Ground-hugging at 6 inches (15 cm) high, thyme has blue flowers that bloom all summer and attract bees. Set plants grown from seeds or cuttings (cuttings are better) 10 inches (25 cm) apart in slightly rich soil that must be well drained, especially during the winter. Thyme leaves are a well-known flavoring in a number of dishes; close relatives are lemon thyme and caraway thyme. Its fragrance also repels cabbage moths.

*Thyme*

184

# Sources of Natural Gardening Supplies

Gardens Alive! Hwy. 48, P.O. Box 149, Sunman, IN 47041

Green Earth Organics, 9422 144th Street E, Puyallup, WA 98373

Growing Naturally, P.O. Box 54, 149 Pine Lane, Pineville, PA 18946

The Natural Gardening Co., 217 San Anselmo Avenue, San Anselmo, CA 94960

Nature Safe, 4221 Alexandria Pike, Cold Spring, KY 41076

Nature's Control, P.O. Box 35, Medford, OR 97501

Necessary Trading Co., One Nature's Way, New Castle, VA 24127

North Country Organics, P.O. Box 107, Newbury, VT 05051

Ringer Corp., 9959 Valley View Road, Eden Prairie, MN 55344

Safer, 189 Wells Avenue, Newton, MA 02159

Walt Nicke Co., 36 McLeod Lane, P.O. Box 433, Topsfield, MA 01983

# 🌿 *Bibliography* 🌿

*An Illustrated Guide to Organic Gardening.* Menlo Park, Calif.: Sunset Books, 1991.

Campbell, Stu. *Let It Rot! The Gardener's Guide to Composting.* Pownal, Vt.: Storey Communications, 1990.

Carr, Anna. *Good Neighbors: Companion Planting for Gardeners.* Emmaus, Pa.: Rodale Press, 1985.

Carr, Anna, et al. *Chemical Free Yard & Garden.* Emmaus, Pa.: Rodale Press, 1991.

Cox, Jeff. *How to Grow Vegetables Organically.* Emmaus, Pa.: Rodale Press, 1988.

Foster, Catherine Osgood. *Building Healthy Gardens.* Pownal, Vt.: Garden Way Publishing, 1989.

Hamilton, Geoff. *The Organic Garden Book.* New York: Crown Publishers, 1987.

*Organic Flower Gardening.* Emmaus, Pa.: Rodale Press, 1975.

Reilly, Ann. *Park's Success with Seeds.* Greenwood, S.C.: Geo. W. Park Seed Co., 1978.

Rodale, Robert. *The Basic Book of Organic Gardening.* New York: Ballantine Books, 1971.

*Rodale's Illustrated Encyclopedia of Herbs.* Emmaus, Pa.: Rodale Press, 1987.

Smith, Miranda, and Anna Carr. *Rodale's Garden Insect, Disease, and Weed Identification Guide.* Emmaus, Pa.: Rodale Press, 1988.

*The Encyclopedia of Organic Gardening.* Emmaus, Pa.: Rodale Press, 1978.

Yepsen, Roger B., Jr., ed. *The Encyclopedia of Natural Insect and Disease Control.* Emmaus, Pa.: Rodale Press, 1984.

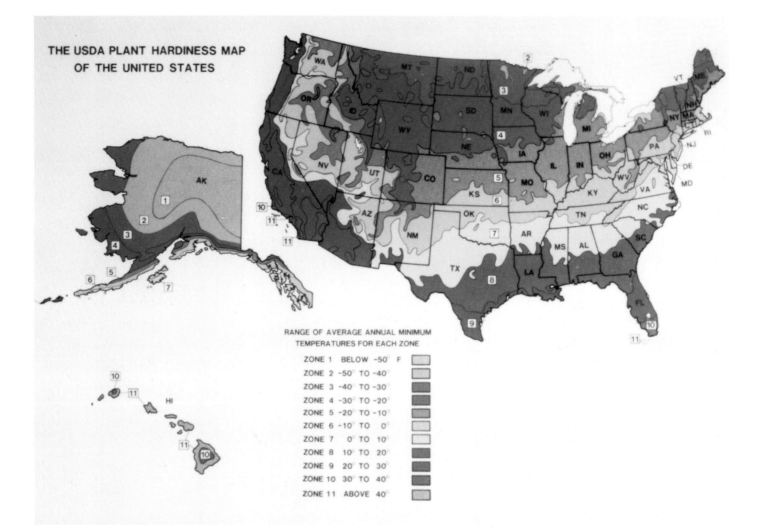

THE USDA PLANT HARDINESS MAP
OF THE UNITED STATES

RANGE OF AVERAGE ANNUAL MINIMUM
TEMPERATURES FOR EACH ZONE

ZONE 1   BELOW -50° F
ZONE 2   -50° TO -40°
ZONE 3   -40° TO -30°
ZONE 4   -30° TO -20°
ZONE 5   -20° TO -10°
ZONE 6   -10° TO   0°
ZONE 7     0° TO  10°
ZONE 8    10° TO  20°
ZONE 9    20° TO  30°
ZONE 10   30° TO  40°
ZONE 11  ABOVE  40°

# ❧ *Index* ❧

## A

*Abelmoschus esculentus*, 54, 148, *148*
*Achillea*, 126
*Ageratum houstonianum*, 67, 116
*Alcea rosea*, 126, *127*
*Allium cepa*, 73, 79, 148
*Allium empeloprasum*, 149
*Allium sativum*, 78, *78*, 149
*Allium schoenoprasum*, 78, 170, *170*
*Aloysia triphylla*, 171
*Anethum graveolens*, 55, 78, 171, *171*
*Angelica archangelica*, 56, 171
Animal control, 97
Anise. *See Pimpinella anisum.*
Annuals, 100, 103, 104, 111, 115
  easy, 116, 117, 119, 120, 121, 123, 124
  fertilizing, 43, 44
  half-hardy, 60, 104, 116, 117, 118, 119, 120, 121, 122, 123, 124
  hardy, 60, 104, 117, 118,
  121, 123, 124
  insect-repelling, 118, 122, 123, 124
  light requirements for, 116–124
  nitrogen-fixing, 121
  soil moisture, 116–124
  temperature require-
    ments for, 116–124
  tender, 104, 119, 120, 121, 122, 123, 124
Anthracnose, 81, 84, *84*
*Anthriscus cerefolium*, 55, 172
Antidesiccants, 83
*Antirrhinum majus*, *59*, 117
Aphids, 76, 77, 78, 79, 80, 81, 82, 83, 86, 87
*Apium graveolens*, 73, 78, 149, *149*
*Arachis hypogaea*, 149
Armoracia rusticana, 79, 150
*Artemisia dracunculus* var. *sativa*, 172
*Asparagus officinalis*, 73, 78, 150
*Aster*, 127

Aster, China. *See Callistephus chinensis.*
Aster yellows, 84, *84*
*Astilbe*, *126*, 127

## B

Bactericides, 81
*Baptisia australis*, 127
Basil. *See Ocimum basilicum.*
Beans
  green. *See Phaseolus vulgaris.*
  lima. *See Phaseolus limensis.*
Beds, raised, 30–31, *143*
Bee balm. *See Monarda didyma.*
Beetles, *74*, 75, 76, 77, 78, 79, 80, 81, 82, 87, *87*
Beets. *See Beta vulgaris.*
*Begonia sempervirens-cultorum*, 67, 117
Bellflower. *See Campanula.*
*Bellis perennis*, 128
*Beta vulgaris*, 150, *151*
Biennials, 104
  light requirements for, 126–137

soil moisture, 126–137
temperature require-
  ments for, 126–137
Birds, 95, 97
Black-eyed Susan. *See Rudbeckia fulgida.*
Blackspot, 74, *85*
Blanketflower. *See Gaillardia pulchella*; *Gaillardia* × *grandiflora.*
Blazing star. *See Liatris spicata.*
Bleeding heart. *See Dicentra.*
Borage. *See Borago officinalis.*
*Borago officinalis*, 55, 78, 172
Bordeaux mixture, 81, 83, 85
Botrytis, 82, 84–85, *85*
*Brassica napus*, 151
*Brassica oleracea*, 117, *150*, 151
*Brassica rapa*, 152
Brussels sprouts, *54*
BT, *81*, 88
Burnet. *See Poterium sanguisorba.*

## C

Cabbage. *See Brassica oleracea.*

Chinese. *See Brassica rapa.*

flowering. *See Brassica oleracea.*

*Calendula officinalis*, 67, 78, 118, *118*

*Callistephus chinensis*, 118

*Campanula*, 128

Candytuft. *See Iberis.*

*Capsicum annuum*, 73, 118, 152, *152*

Caraway. *See Carum carvi.*

Carcinogens, 10

Carrot. *See Daucus carota.*

Carson, Rachel, 9

*Carum carvi*, 55, *172*, 173

Caterpillars, 76, 77, 81, 88, *88*

*Catharanthus roseus*, 26, 67, 118

Catnip. *See Nepeta cataria.*

Celery. *See Apium graveolens.*

Cell packs, 60

*Celosia cristata*, 119

*Chamaemelum nobile*, 173

Chamomile

Russian. *See Chamaemelum nobile.*

sweet false. *See Matricaria recutita.*

Charcoal, activated, 12

*Chelone lyonii*, 128

Chervil. *See Anthriscus cerefolium.*

Chipmunks, 97

Chives. *See Allium schoenoprasum.*

Chlorosis, 47, *47*

*Chrysanthemum*, 128

*Cichorium endivia*, 152, *153*

Cilantro. *See Coriandrum sativum.*

*Citrullus lanatus*, 152–153

*Cleome hasslerana*, 119

Cockscomb. *See Celosia cristata.*

Cold frame, *19*, 67–68

*Coleus × hybridus*, 67, 119

Compost, 19, *19*, 20, *21*, *22*, 22–23, 29, 55

activators, *22*

sheeting, 24

Coneflower, purple. *See Echinacea purpurea.*

Copper sulfate, 81, 84

*Coreopsis*, *128*, 129

Coriander. *See Coriandrum sativum.*

*Coriandrum sativum*, 55, 78, 173, *173*

Corn. *See Zea mays.*

*Cosmos bipinnatus*, 119, *119*

*Cosmos sulphureus*, 119, *119*

Cranesbill. *See Geranium.*

Crop rotation, 10, 76, 85, 86, 144, 148, 152, 156

Cucumber. *See Cucumis sativus.*

*Cucumis melo*, 54, 55, 75, 153

*Cucumis sativus*, 55, 73, 153

*Cucurbita*, 75, 154, *154*, *155*

Cumin. *See Cuminum cyminum.*

*Cuminum cyminum*, 173

Cuttings, 58–59

## D

Daisy

English. *See Bellis perennis.*

gloriosa. *See Rudbeckia hirta.*

Damping off, 55, 85

*Daucus carota*, 154

Daylily. *See Hemerocallis.*

DDT, 9, 10

Dead-heading, 67

*Delphinium*, 56, 129, *129*

*Dianthus chinensis*, 120

Diatomaceous earth, 81, 87, 88, 90

*Dicentra*, 130, *130*

Dieback, 46

*Digitalis purpurea*, *111*, 130, *131*

Dill. *See Anethum graveolens.*

Disease

controlling, 73–74, 83–86

milky spore, 81, 87, 92

resistance to, 12, 16, 35, 37, 150, 151, 153, 157, 158, 159

soilborne, 18, 22, 76, 86

Divisions, 59

Dormant feeding, 44, 46

Dormant oil, 81, 84, 87

*Dracocephalum virginianum*, 130

Drainage, 10, 12, 17, 18, 29, 30–31, 54, 85

Drought resistance, 16, 54

Dusty miller, 26, *27*

## E

Earthworms, 12, 18, 24–25

*Echinops ritro*, 132, *132*

Eggplant. *See Solanum melongena.*

*Echinacea purpurea*, 130

Endive. *See Cichorium endivia.*

Escarole. *See Cichorium endivia.*

## F

False dragonhead. *See Dracocephalum virginianum.*

Fennel. *See Foeniculum vulgare.*
Fertilizer, 17, 18, 28, 33–49, 172
  complete, 35, 46
  inorganic, 37
  natural, 16, 40, 42
  organic, 36
  pH, 39
  timing, 43
  use, 43–46
Fish emulsion, 36, 37, 38, 40, 43, 56, 172
Floss flower. *See Ageratum houstonianum.*
Flowering tobacco. *See Nicotiana alata.*
*Foeniculum vulgare,* 55, 174, *174*
Foxglove. *See Digitalis purpurea.*
Fungicides, 81, 83, 92–93
Funkia. *See Hosta.*

**G**

*Gaillardia pulchella,* 120
*Gaillardia* × *grandiflora,* 132
*Galium odoratum,* 174
Garden
  beds, *44*
  color selection, 112–113, 115
  container, 39, 43, 68, 69, *103,* 111
  cutting, 109
  design, 106–115, 141–145, 164
  flower, 102–116
  herb, 162–169
  vegetable, 140–147
Garlic. *See Allium sativum.*
*Gazania rigens,* 120
*Geranium,* 26, *27,* 56, 132, *133. See also Pelargonium.*
Globeflower. *See Trollius europaeus.*
Globe thistle. *See Echinops ritro.*
Goldenrod. *See Solidago.*
Gophers, 97
Gray mold, 84–85
Greenhouse, *55,* 56, 57
Grubs, 81
Gypsum, 31, 47

**H**

Hardening off, 46, 56, 57
Hard pan, 31
Heaving, 67
*Helianthus annuus,* 120, *120*
*Helleborus,* 132
*Hemerocallis,* 132
Herbicides, 9
Herbs, 161–183
  drying, 168–169
  fertilizing, 43, 44
  insect repelling, 170, 171, 173, 176, 177, 180, 181, 182, 183
  invasive, 164, 176
Hollyhock. *See Alcea rosea.*
Horseradish. *See Armoracia rusticana.*
*Hosta,* 133
Hot bed, 67–68
Howard, Sir Albert, 10
Humus, 18, 28
Hyacinths, *68*
*Hysoppus officinalis,* 174

**I**

*Iberis,* 65, 120
*Impatiens wallerana,* 67, 121
Indigo, blue false. *See Baptisia australis.*
Insecticides, 10, 92–93
  contact, 87
  natural, 75, 80–83
Insect(s)
  beneficial, 74, 76–77
  control, 74–75, 80–83
  predatory, 12, 76–77, 87, 89, 91
  resistance to, 16, 35, 118, 122, 123, 124, 170, 171, 173, 176, 177, 180, 181, 182, 183
  vegetable, 148, 150, 151, 152, 153, 154, 155, 157, 158, 159
Interplanting, 144, 157, 171, 172
*Ipomoea,* 121, *121*
*Ipomoea batatas,* 55, 73, 75, 155
*Iris* × *germanica, 21, 104,* 133

**K**

Kale. *See Brassica oleracea.*

**L**

*Lactuca sativa, 16, 73, 75, 142,* 155
*Lavandula angustifolia,* 175
Lavender. *See Lavandula angustifolia.*
Lavender cotton. *See Santolina chamaecyparissus.*
Leaf
  mold, 20, *21,* 29, 55
  spot, 81, 82, 85
Leafhoppers, 76, 78, 79, 81, 82, 83, 84, 88
Leeks. *See Allium empeloprasum.*
Lemon
  balm. *See Melissa officinalis.*
  verbena. *See Aloysia triphylla.*
Lettuce. *See Lactuca sativa.*

*Levisticum officinale*, 175
*Liatris spicata*, 134
Light requirements
    for annuals, 116–124
    for biennials, 126–137
    for perennials, 126–137
Lily, plantain. *See Hosta.*
Limestone, 39, 47
*Lobelia*, 65, 67, 121
*Lobularia maritima*, 65,
    67, 121
Lovage. *See Levisticum
    officinale.*
*Lupinus*, 134, *134*
*Lycopersicon lysopersicum*,
    *56*, *73*, *75*, *79*, *148*,
    156
*Lythrum salicaria*, 135

## M
Maggots, 77, 79, 81, 83,
    88
Manure, 20, 22, 23, 29,
    38, 40
    green, 24
    tea, 39
Marigold
    African. *See Tagetes
        erecta.*
    French. *See Tagetes
        patula.*
    pot. *See Calendula
        officinalis.*
Marjoram, sweet. *See
    Origanum majorana.*

*Matricaria recutita*, 175,
    *175*
Meal
    blood, 37, 40, 42, 97
    bone, 30, 36, 38, 39, 40,
        42, 43, 46, 83, 97
    cottonseed, 36, 38, 40
    fish, 37, 38, 41
Mealybugs, 76, 77, 81, 83,
    88, *89*
*Melissa officinalis*, 176
Melon. *See Cucumis melo.*
*Mentha*, 79, 176
Mice, 97
Mildew, 74, 81, 82, 84, 85,
    110, 124, 135, 155
    downy, 150, 153
Mint. *See Mentha.*
Mites, 76, 77, 78, 79, 81,
    82, 83, 87, 89
Moles, 97
*Monarda didyma*, 176, *176*
Morning glory. *See
    Ipomoea.*
Mosaic, 85–86
Moss rose. *See Portulaca
    grandiflora.*
Mulch, 62, 63–64, 74, 87
    decorative, 64
    natural, 63
    plastic, 64, *64*
    seaweed, *38*

## N
Nasturtium. *See
    Tropaeolum majus.*
*Nasturtium officinale*, 177
Nematodes, 76, 77, 78,
    79, 89
*Nepeta cataria*, 78, 177
*Nicotiana alata*, 122, *122*
Nicotine sulfate, 81
Nitrogen, 22, 23, 24, 35,
    37, 46, 47, 49
Nutrient deficiency, 48–
    49

## O
*Ocimum basilicum*, 177,
    *177*
Okra. *See Abelmoschus
    esculentus.*
Onion. *See Allium cepa.*
Oregano. *See Origanum.*
*Origanum*, 178, *178*
*Origanum majorana*, 178
Overfertilizing, 46
Oyster shells, 27, 39, 47

## P
*Paeonia officinalis*, 135, *135*
Pansy. *See Viola ×
    wittrockiana.*
*Papaver orientalis*, 104, 135
Parsley. *See Petroselinum
    crispum.*
Parsnip. *See Pastinaca
    sativa.*

*Pastinaca sativa*, 73, 156
Peanuts. *See Arachis
    hypogaea.*
Peas. *See Pisum sativum.*
Peat moss, 19, 20, 29, 54,
    55, 56, 63, 68
*Pelargonium*, 178
*Pelargonium × hortorum*,
    122
Peony. *See Paeonia
    officinalis.*
Peppers. *See Capsicum
    annuum.*
Perennials, 100, 103, 104,
    115
    dormant feeding, 44, 46
    easy, 126, 127, 128, 129,
        130, 132, 133, 134,
        136, 137
    fertilizing, 43, 44, 46
    light requirements, 126–
        137
    soil moisture, 126–137
    temperature require-
        ments for, 126–137
    transplanting, 55
Periwinkle. *See
    Catharanthus roseus.*
Perlite, 25, 55, 68
Pesticides, 9, 12
*Petroselinum crispum*, 55,
    73, 179, *179*
*Petunia × hybrida*, 61, *61*,
    79, 122
*Phaseolus limensis*, 75, 156

*Phaseolus vulgaris*, 73, 78, 157

Pheromone, 80

*Phlox drummondi*, 123

*Phlox paniculata*, 135

*Phlox subulata*, 66

Phosphorus, 27, 30, 35, 36, 37, 38, 39, 46, 47, 49

Photosynthesis, 35

*Pimpinella anisum*, 55, 78, 180

Pink, China. *See Dianthus chinensis.*

*Pisum sativum*, 24, 58, 73, 157

Planting, 60–61
  companion, 12, 78–79, 97

Plant selection, 52–54, 60
  environmental requirements, 54
  light requirements, 54

Poppy, Oriental. *See Papaver orientalis.*

*Portulaca grandiflora*, 54, 123

Potassium, 27, 35, 36, 37, 46, 47, 49

Potato. *See Solanum tuberosum.*

*Poterium sanguisorba*, 180

Potpourri, 169, 171, 175, 181

*Primula*, 111, 136

Proportioner, 43, 91

Pruning, 65, 67, 84, 85, 86, 89

Pumpkin. *See Cucurbita.*

Purple loosestrife. *See Lythrum salicaria.*

Pyrethrum, 10, 75, 82, 87, 88

**R**

Rabbits, 78, 97, 170

Radish. *See Raphanus sativus.*

*Raphanus sativus*, 54, 75, 79, 157, *157*

*Rheum rhabarbarum*, 158, *158*

Rhubarb. *See Rheum rhabarbarum.*

Rock
  phosphate, 30, 39, 41, 46
  powder, 36

Rodale, Jerome, 9, 10

Rodent control, 97

Rose, Christmas. *See Helleborus.*

Rose, Lenten. *See Helleborus.*

Rosemary. *See Rosmarinus officinalis.*

*Rosmarinus officinalis*, 79, *79*, 181

Rotenone, 10, 82, 87, 88, 89

*Rudbeckia fulgida*, 136, *137*

*Rudbeckia hirta*, 123, *123*

Rue. *See Ruta graveolens.*

Rust, 81, 86, 126

Rutabaga. *See Brassica napus.*

*Ruta graveolens*, 79, 181

**S**

Sabadilla, 82, 88

Sage. *See Salvia officinalis.*
  scarlet. *See Salvia splendens.*

*Salvia officinalis*, 79, 181, *181*

*Salvia splendens*, 123

*Santolina chamaecyparissus*, *180*, 181

*Sanvitalia procumbens*, 55, 123

*Satureja*, 79, 182

Savory. *See Satureja.*

Scab, 82, 83, 86

Scale, 77, 81, *82*, 83, 89

Scarecrows, *96*, 97

Seaweed, 38, 41, 43
  mulch, *38*

*Sedum*, 136

Seeds, 54–59
  germination, 55
  light requirements for, 55, 56, 58
  soaking, 56, 59
  sowing, 55, 56, 58

transplanting, 56

Side dressing, *21*

Slips, 155

Slugs, 79, 87, *89*, 89–90

Snails, 79, 87, 89–90

Snapdragon. *See Antirrhinum majus.*

Soil, 17, *18*
  acidic, 18, 25, 26–27, 31
  aeration, 10, 17, 18, 30–31
  alkaline, 18, 19, 25, 26, 28, 31, 47, 129, 133, 180
  amendments, 18–23, 39, 42, 46, 47, 48
  clay, *17*, 18, 25
  improvement, 12, 28–30
  loam, *17*, 18
  moisture requirements, 116–137
  organic, 16, 18–23
  pH, 18, 19, 20, 25, 26–28, 43, 47, 48, 74, 146, 150, 153
  problems, 31
  replacement, 86
  sandy, 17, *17*, 18, 28
  silt, *17*, 18
  structure, 17–18, 24, 48, 63
  testing, 26, 43, 46, *46*, 47, 48
  texture, 17–18

*Solanum melongena*, 73, 158, *158*

*Solanum tuberosum*, 73, 79, 158

*Solidago*, 136

Speedwell. *See Veronica spicata.*

Spider flower. *See Cleome hasslerana.*

Spinach. *See Spinacia oleracea.*

New Zealand. *See Tetragonia tetragonoides.*

*Spinacia oleracea*, 159, *159*

Sprayers, 91, *92*

Spraying, 92–95

Squash. *See Cucurbita.*

Squirrels, 97

Staking, *64*, 65, 168

Sticky cards, 80, *82*, 88

Stonecrop. *See Sedum.*

Sulfur, 47, 82–83, 83, 85, 87, 89

agricultural, 28

elemental, 85

lime, 81, 83, 85, 86, 89, 91

Summer oil, 83

Sunflower. *See Helianthus annuus.*

Sweet alyssum. *See Lobularia maritima.*

Sweet potato. *See Ipomoea batatas.*

Sweet woodruff. *See Galium odoratum.*

Swiss chard. *See Beta vulgaris.*

**T**

*Tagetes erecta*, 60, 123

*Tagetes patula*, 124

*Tanacetum vulgare*, 79, 182, 183

Tansy. *See Tanacetum vulgare.*

Tarragon, French. *See Artemisia dracunculus* var. *sativa.*

Temperature requirements for annuals, 116–125

for biennials, 126–137

for perennials, 126–137

Tepees, 65, *65*

*Tetragonia tetragonoides*, 159

Thinning out, 56, 58

Thrips, 76, 80, 81, 91

Thyme. *See Thymus vulgaris.*

*Thymus vulgaris*, 26, 79, 183, *183*

Tickseed. *See Coreopsis.*

Tobacco mosaic virus, 82

Tomato. *See Lycopersicon lysopersicum.*

Tools, *52*

Trace elements, 47–48

Transplanting, 55, 56

Trap plants, 80

Traps, 80, *80*, *81*, 86, 87, 88, 90, 97

Treasure flower. *See Gazania rigens.*

Trellises, 65, 109, *109*

*Trillium*, 136

*Trollius europaeus*, 136

*Tropaeolum majus*, 55, 79, 124, *125*

Tulips, *68*, *115*

Turtlehead. *See Chelone lyonii.*

**U**

Urea, 36

**V**

Vegetables, 139–159

bolt-resistant, 159

climate requirements, 148–159

disease resistant, *72*, 73, 150, 151, 153, 157, 158, 159

**W**

Wake robin. *See Trillium.*

Wasps, 76, 77

Watercress. *See Nasturtium officinale.*

Watering, 61–62, *95*

bottom, 56

drip irrigation, 62, 73

hand, 62, *62*

night, 85

overhead, 62

Watermelon. *See Citrullus lanatus.*

Weeds, 6, 74, 86, 88

Wilt, 86, *86*, 155

Winter protection, 21, 67, 97, 104, *146*, 168

Wood ashes, 20, 27, 38, 41, 43, 83

**Y**

Yarrow. *See Achillea.*

**Z**

*Zea mays*, 55, 73, 75, 159

Zinnia, creeping. *See Sanvitalia procumbens.*

*Zinnia elegans*, 124